The Kennedy Legacy: It's Time to Fulfill It

The Kennedy Legacy: It's Time to Fulfill It

The Demise of American Culture and How to Revive It

Linda Rae Hermann

Writers Club Press

San Jose New York Lincoln Shanghai

The Kennedy Legacy: It's Time to Fulfill It
The Demise of American Culture and How to Revive It

Published by Writers Club Press
an imprint of iUniverse.com, Inc.

For information address:
iUniverse.com, Inc.
620 North 48th Street
Suite 201
Lincoln, NE 68504-3467
www.iuniverse.com

ISBN: 0-595-09884-3

Printed in the United States of America

Dedication

This book is dedicated to the memory of John F. Kennedy, who tried to preserve our hereditary culture, the public philosophy, by calling American citizens to unselfish service and to the children who have died at the hands of other children because the public philosophy was not passed on.

Epigraph

To restore the public philosophy to our nation, Americans need to seek in our heritage the truths that laid its foundation. We must find the God-Formed and self-evident truths that all people are created for a purpose, and that purpose is to contribute to and serve one's family, one's neighbors, one's community, and one's nation. We are endowed with duties to protect individual rights and promote the common good. We are called to cultivate the qualities and habits of good character, giving ourselves over to forming an upright conscience and living by the highest moral principles of love, courage, and duty. We must take up the standard raised by John F. Kennedy and finally answer his summons to ask how we can serve our country and its citizens rather than ask how we can be served. That is the Kennedy legacy, and it is time to fulfill it.

Table of Contents

Preface

I was a teenager in the 1950s. I loved my country, and I was one of those idealistic teenagers who felt a deep desire to go into public service. I identified with those who were suffering injustices at that time, and I wanted to right some of those wrongs. In college, I continued to pursue this goal and majored in political science. I intended to go to Georgetown University or attend law school after receiving my BA. Then I planned to live in a poor area from which I would run for office and help the disadvantaged.

In my senior year of college, I had a revelation that changed all of my plans. On taking a course in business ethics, I was exposed to corruption and deception previously unknown to me. As a result of reflecting on ethical misconduct in business, I related this conduct to politics. I concluded that the political realm must be equally or more corrupted than business. I concluded I was too naïve to consider a political career until I had laid a stronger moral foundation. I did not want to become a public servant, and end up being a corrupt and immoral one, unable to represent those most in need.

I sensed at that time, a movement in politics towards greater greed, corruption, and competition. As a result of my realization about my weaknesses and the weaknesses of the system, I set off to find a way to grow in character and ethical clarity. Instead of attending law school, I converted to Catholicism and began graduate studies in theology. After a year of taking classes towards a Masters in theology, I returned to California to enter a religious order. I was especially looking for solace and purpose since John F. Kennedy, whose message of service had increased my hunger to serve my country, was assassinated that previous year. His death made me even more aware of the precarious state of our nation morally and politically.

During the time I entered the convent, in 1964, Pope John XXIII began to reform the Catholic Church. It was the beginning of a liberalization of the Church, which resulted in tremendous tension in the religious community I joined. By the end of two years, when I left, the order was ready to split between the reformers and traditionalists. I had learned more about God and morality, but I did not find the suitable place to which I could contribute my talents.

Upon leaving the religious order, I was drawn to the Hippie Movement just beginning in San Francisco. I had read about it while in the convent. By then, 1966, my disillusionment had developed into despair. I searched to put meaning to all I had learned and seen. The Hippie idea, "to drop out," fit my feelings of powerlessness to be able to do anything to help my country and its citizens. In a state of confusion and despair, I joined others in the Haight-Ashbury of San Francisco. I identified with their criticism of our materialistic and hypocritical society.

By the end of the summer of 1967, the Hippie community in San Francisco self-destructed. My husband and I had gone to New York City in the summer of 1967 to get away from the dissolving movement and the destruction by drugs of many of our friends. When we returned in 1968, most of our friends and other Hippies had left the city to go live in the country. We remained in San Francisco and started a family until 1972.

In 1972, we moved to a farming community in northern California near Eureka. There I continued to search to establish some meaning out of my experiences and the national transformation that was occurring. Soon after arriving in the countryside, we met a preacher who was forming a new church. He was reaching out to the lost people of that period, and it was part of a bigger movement, called the Jesus Movement. We spent twelve years with that pastor. We lived communally and gave ourselves to complete spiritual saturation. There were many excesses in this Christian community, but it provided a structured, clearly defined environment in which to grow spiritually and morally.

Up until 1989, I had concentrated upon raising my family, serving in my church, and growing in ethical knowledge. In 1989, the year the Berlin Wall fell, I returned to college to begin my studies for my Masters in political science. I reentered the secular world and the world of education with a desire to understand why the United States was in a worse state than when I left it (in my mind), in 1964.

It was then, in 1989, that I began to develop the themes and thesis for this book. Since then, all of my activities, thoughts, and studying have gone into formulating the ideas in this book. I have spent these many years watching and experiencing the upheavals and cultural revolution that has occurred in our society. I have lived through and participated in that revolution while also viewing it as an observer. My goal has been during these years since 1964 to become a morally upright person who could continue to identify with her fellow man and discover some answers that could help restore our culture to ethical clarity and political well-being.

As I returned to college and invested my free time in helping in my community, it came to me that I was ethically prepared to enter public service. In 1998, I ran for the office of school board trustee in San Jose, California, and was elected. I have now begun the service I intended to do over thirty-five years ago. Whether I remain politically active locally or go beyond the local area is uncertain. Most importantly, I hope to have influence on the minds of Americans through this book, which has had an extremely long period of incubation.

For the readers of this book, I hope it does all that I have intended it to do. I hope it opens your eyes to the revolution that has taken place in our nation. I want you to know that there has been a revolution, and it has changed the character of America. It is up to you to make a decision whether you want our nation to remain true to its ethical and political roots, or if you prefer our nation to be a completely different culture than our Founding Fathers' created and intended.

It has been said that without knowledge people perish. I am trying to give the Americans who read this book the knowledge they need to make a choice. Up until the present time, forces in our society have moved deceptively to undertake radical changes. Such important changes should be decided by citizens not an elite. Now that you will know the past, the present, and the future plans of those in power, you can choose how you can best serve our nation. Hopefully, you will decide to move this country down the path to cultural restoration.

Acknowledgements

I am grateful to my good friend, Sherri Cook, who labored tirelessly over a period of many months, reading and re-reading the initial manuscript. She served as my editor and confidant. Without her, parts of this book would have been awkward or grammatically questionable. She gave herself to this endeavor with enthusiasm and vigor, which I could never repay with sufficient money or gratitude.

Also, I must thank my husband, Ed, who read over the book as it was being written and then, the completed manuscript. He was steadfast in his support and suggestions. He spent many hours with our dog, Lucky, as a substitute for my presence. I will always be grateful for his enthusiasm about my ideas, and his willingness to sacrifice our time together for the fulfillment of my dream.

Chapter 1.

The Demise of American Culture

What Has Been The Heart
Of American Culture?

To say that the demise of American culture is a reality may be an over-statement, but if the original American culture is not dead, then it is on its deathbed. In order to prove that statement we must first know what is meant by culture? Culture is a combination of the customs, norms, values, institutions, traditions, habits, manners, skills, art, etc., of a given people at a given time. The foundational culture of America was formed by the influence of the Puritan-Pilgrim settlers and the Founding Fathers, which was in turn, influenced by a blend of Enlightenment philosophy, Protestant faith, and New World experiences. This uniquely American culture has been the bedrock of our distinct republican, democratic form of government and of our brand of western civilization.

Thomas Jefferson expressed this foundational blend when he wrote the Declaration of Independence. In it he defended the right of America to separate from England because "the Laws of Nature and of Nature's God entitle them,…" Then he went on to write that famous passage: "We hold these truths to be self-evident, that all men are created equal, that they are endowed by their Creator with certain unalienable rights, that among these are life, liberty, and the pursuit of happiness." Jefferson looked to God and Nature for the absolute, universal, first-principles upon which and from which all rights were derived.

It was this Judeo-Christian and Enlightenment thinking that created the firm, cultural foundation upon which future generations would build a unique form of American government and culture. With this foundation, the United States of America was able to absorb the cultures of many immigrant populations without losing its own unique identity. It was able to provide a balance of liberty and equality to the common man, which had never been known in the history of the world. The cultural foundation created by early Americans was the source of the stable government that has survived, with varying degrees of success, up until the present day.

American cultural heritage has various names. In this book, borrowing terminology from Walter Lippmann, it will be called "the public philosophy" or "the traditions of civility." Our cultural heritage, the public philosophy, has given America a specific world view. Early Americans, more than any other people in the history of the world, had an opportunity to consciously create a new kind of country with a new kind of government. The majority of first settlers, being able to read, having considerable manners, having religious fervor, having independence from the mother-land, and having an educated, middle class mentality; provided the seeds for the future success of the American experiment.

The public philosophy that evolved from the 1620 to 1776 was based upon the premise, or first-principle, that human nature consisted of a mixture of good and evil tendencies. They logically concluded from this premise that the evil part of human nature needed to be restrained and contained by certain civilizing traditions and institutions. To our ancestors, a civilized society needed to possess clearly defined manners and moral absolutes guiding behavior; government institutions containing checks and balances on human nature; public servants influenced by religion; customs, traditions, and mores guiding daily interactions; and a set of just laws to define and punish illegal behavior. Our founders understanding of the good and evil capacity of human nature laid the foundation for our form of government and the American culture.

The consequences for right or wrong were clearly defined in early America. Right behavior was rewarded and wrong behavior was punished. For that reason, there was very little crime in the colonies. It would have been unthinkable to talk back to an adult, show disrespect for any person, swear in public, steal, and take another person's life. The poor were provided for as long as they were willing to work. A stranger was provided with a place to eat and sleep when traveling. Although the Puritans were at times, overbearing and self-righteous, overall, they were loving and kind. Although at times, condemning and rigid, their insight into the makeup of human nature was accurate. Although the Puritan approach was softened by the time of the Founding Fathers, still these men agreed with them that the character qualities of honesty, respect, responsibility, fairness, justice, patience, kindness, love, and forgiveness were not natural to humans without rewards, punishments, customs, moral absolutes, traditions, manners, institutions and religion. Therefore, they planted the public philosophy deep into American consciousness and into its institutions, which has enabled America to retain more liberty than most, if not all, nations without falling into anarchy or dictatorship.

A Need For The Public Philosophy

Since the beginning of the Industrial Revolution in the late nineteenth century, America has been in a struggle to preserve the traditional philosophy on which freedom and self-government depend. The survival of the republican form of government created by our Founding Fathers depends upon a specific philosophical and cultural belief system. There are aspects of it that can be adjusted and revised as our culture changes, but there are some elements of the traditional views that must remain.

The reason our traditional worldview, public philosophy, must prevail in American society is because it contains the values and virtues that prevent democracies from declining and which maintain a civilized society. Lippmann, a philosopher and journalist, wrote in 1955 that "Underlying the present critical condition of western society is the fact that the democracies are ceasing to receive those traditions of civility in which the good society, or the liberal democratic way of life at its best, originated and developed…traditions of civility are the art of government and principles for human conduct that are founded in natural law and transcend human conception."[1]

In 1955 Walter Lippmann made the case that America was nearly devoid of the knowledge and practice of the public philosophy, and for that reason we were experiencing the loss of freedom and self-government. Before further describing that philosophy, we need to see if there are signs in America, which reveal we have lost the means by which to preserve our democratic republic and maintain civility in our society. Do we have signs of decline? Do American citizens have less power over their government, and have they become more uncivilized? If we find the answer to these questions is yes, then, in a search for the cause of our civil decline, we can analyze the traditional American worldview and compare it to our present worldview.

The Decline Of Self-Rule, Nationally

Let us look at some examples of the decline of self-rule by American citizens. Do American citizens make their will known to the government, and do their representatives act upon their will? On the federal level there are many examples of Congress and/or the President acting without hearing or asking for the will of the people.

One recent example of the use of unlimited power by the Executive Branch was the Kosovo War. According to Article One, Section Eight of the Constitution, only Congress has the power to declare war. The Executive Branch can only repel "sudden attacks. The War Powers Resolution passed in 1973 to reassert the power of Congress to declare war, requires the president to "make a formal report to Congress within 48 hours of sending U.S. military forces equipped for combat into foreign territory or a situation in which hostilities are likely."[2] President Bill Clinton and other presidents since 1973 have denied the presence of hostilities or called the war by another name, such as a conflict. The bombing of Kosovo did not fit the definition of either the Constitution or the War Powers Resolution; and yet, neither the President nor the Secretary of Defense formally reported to Congress or consulted with Congress. There was political debate only because some congressional members forced the issue onto the floor of the House of Representatives.

Using NATO was a convenient way for the Executive Branch to circumvent a congressional decision, public debate, and the role of the United Nations. NATO, created for the protection of Western Europe during the Cold War, has been maintained since the end of the Cold War. This European, military coalition allows the Executive Branch, the President and his department heads, to have more independent power in the international arena. Under the auspices of NATO, presidents can claim that a war is not an American war. It is a joint military action of Europe and the United States. The Constitution and the War Powers Resolution did not foresee this new configuration of a coalition exercising military power outside of national constitutional constraints.

Through maneuvering, Clinton was able to avoid the checks and balances provided by Congress and public opinion. The public remained completely passive during the Kosovo War, even though Clinton never described the purpose or need for the war in great detail. There was no need to influence public opinion because citizens had learned to let their leaders tell them how to think. The late C. Wright Mills, a Professor of Sociology at Columbia University, wrote in his controversial book, The Power Elite, "the public of public opinion has become the object of intensive efforts to control, manage, manipulate, and increasingly intimidate."[3]

Another aspect of unlimited political power is the decision made by the government concerning which countries received Most Favored

Nation trade status. The continuing trade with China is one of the more obvious decisions made without soliciting public opinion. Many politicians could have made a strong case against extending China Most Favored Nation status, especially with all of the suspicions about their campaign finance contributions and nuclear spy activities. Instead, no leaders, Democratic or Republican, brought the public into that debate. Most congressional members supported corporate, global goals. For a number of years corporations have seen China as a rich field for expanding their wealth and power. The rise of international corporations and the global economy have introduced a new piece into the economic mix. Many global corporations have more income and employees than some cities and/or countries. Many corporations have the power of a country without the limitations of international customs and laws to control them. Corporations, more than the public, influenced the decisions on which nations should receive Most Favored Nation trade status.

Although many politicians influence more than listen to public opinion, in some areas, they actually seek the public viewpoint, such as decisions about taxes and the budget or whether to run for office. Of course, they are always interested to know if voters will vote for them. They seek advice from consultants on what they should say to acquire votes. In those cases, they depend on polls. In spite of the fact that the public has influence on some issues, if those in power choose to manipulate public opinion to their liking, their consciences do not interfere with them using psychology and deception to accomplish that purpose.

Because of the use of polls, there is a belief by some politicians and political analysts that the American representative system is changing to a form of direct democracy, a plebiscite. In direct democracy the people make the policies and laws rather than representatives. With the use of polls, it appears the people have more power in daily governing, but it is not true. Since special interests have a deep understanding of how to sway public opinion by using the media, they strongly influence the thinking of the people who are polled. The media also influences public opinion, depending upon which political ideas it advocates. Often, when the public does have an authentic, self-derived opinion, those in power ignore and confuse the public to avoid accountability.

Political consultants develop a complete strategy to move the public's will to support particular candidates or issues. For example, Clinton used this technique masterfully when he was trying to survive the Lewinsky scandal. Nightly, he sent out his spokespersons to tell people how to think. Most of the time his defenders blamed conspirators, using the appearance of martyrdom to rally the protective instincts of the public. Clinton has always depended upon the appearance of vulnerability to win the public's and women's affections and protection. Hillary Clinton revealed the power of that image when she forgave her husband for his infidelity because of his troubled upbringing. The other nightly strategy of the President's defenders was to appeal to the public's fear of economic disruption; they claimed that character did not matter because Clinton was doing a good job (economically) as President.

The Decline Of Self-Rule, Locally

Because I am the president of a local neighborhood group, I have seen some local trends that threaten to exclude citizens from making decisions that impact their quality of life. I live in San Jose, California, which is part of Silicon Valley. City and county officials have been entering into partnerships with environmental organizations, and high tech corporations in order to solve some local problems. This is a practice occurring in most urban and suburban areas throughout the country. It is an especially prominent activity in areas in which the high tech industry is prospering and expanding.

Although the high tech industry is becoming more aware of its duties to the communities in which they are located, they have not steeped themselves in the republican, democratic way to fulfill their duties. They have formulated plans with county and city officials to improve traffic flow, lower smog emissions, and provide housing, yet officials and business executives have not presented the long-range plan to the citizens. Instead, they have used ill-defined, advisory ballot measures to win approval for their projects without honestly presenting all of the ramifications of their projects.

For example, in the part of the city in which I live, the county transportation department is planning to provide a light rail down a residential, high-traffic street. The citizens of the county approved an advisory measure to develop various forms of transportation to improve traffic flow throughout the area. Now that the plan is being implemented in our neighborhood, local citizens see some major problems: homes along that street will lose property value, the three to four year construction upheaval could put many merchants out of business, there is a potential for flooding, and school-aged children having to cross the rails would be at risk. Moreover, it is uncertain that sufficient numbers of commuters would switch from car to light rail to warrant the reconfiguration of the neighborhood.

Even more important is the recent revelation that local, high-employment computer companies have actually proposed the light rail as part of a larger design. These high tech companies need residences for their employees, but environmentalists are fighting to stop urban sprawl. They are creating a "greenline" around San Jose to stop urban expansion. To solve the high-tech needs and environmental goal, they have joined with the city and county governments to develop high-density housing (the city will go up rather than grow out). In the long run, they want developers to buy up the houses, lots, and orchards along the residential, light rail corridors, and build high-density housing in the place of the present individual family homes. In which case, the light rail will not actually solve the transportation problem because the many new high-density houses will increase the population of our area. The population will far exceed any reduction in traffic brought by light rail.

Their plan might be something that the citizens in the local neighborhoods and throughout the county would support if they saw it as the only means to maintain economic prosperity. However, the real problem is that the details of the bigger plan have not been presented to the public. They have only been told about individual projects. Citizens have been told that the light rail will improve traffic flow without being told that the high-density housing along the light rail will increase traffic problems. In addition, at the meetings held to answer questions and inform the public, no county or city official would answer any questions. Instead, officials asked for questions and comments to be put into the record and then answered in writing through the mail. Because the elected representatives are in partnership with industry, they are failing to inform citizens of the larger picture and to ask for the will of the majority, and they are failing to make the bureaucratic department of transportation follow a democratic process.

Public officials and special interests often justify their undemocratic actions by defending their motives. They often claim they are making decisions that are beneficial to the people they represent, which fits into the practice of justifying the means by a supposed virtuous end. They believe they know best what is good for the residents in the county and its cities. In the case of the light rail and the plan for high-density housing, there are other possible solutions: Corporations could build their companies in neighboring areas, which have potential employable populations living nearby. Expansion into other cities and counties could lighten the traffic problems and restore reasonable housing costs to Silicon Valley. In addition, some of the land being preserved by environmentalists could be used for residential housing. Frequently, environmentalists are more concerned about preserving the quality of life of animals and ecosystems than the quality of life of humans. Therefore, they become immoderate in their environmental solutions.

Having these partnerships of public officials, developers, environmentalists, and industrialists making decisions without public participation is unethical and undemocratic; what is needed is for there to be a public debate about the various options facing citizens. Elected officials should build consensus among the voters, not their partners. In fact, the voters are the most important partners. They are the ones to ultimately decide and pay for the projects. Sadly, in the current situation, they are being excluded, misinformed and/or manipulated.

Although many of the managers and executives in the computer industry see themselves as community-minded and idealistic visionaries, there could also be a case made that they are only a better public relations version of the railroad barons of the late nineteenth and early twentieth centuries. The railroad magnets "partnered" with public officials and government agencies as well. Together they seized many acres of private property in order to expand the railroad across the country.

Moreover, there are some other comparisons that can be made between early factories, which overworked their employees, demanding long hours of work, and high tech industries. It is common knowledge that in the computer industry, employees are expected to give more than forty hours a week to their employers. They are paid well, but many employees go unpaid for the time they put in over a regular forty-hour week. Because it is not physical labor and because many employees enjoy the challenge and creativity of their jobs, they do not relate their unpaid overtime to earlier industrial abuses. They need to stop and analyze their situation and recognize the manipulation that is causing them to sacrifice so much of their time to this industry.

The package may look different, but if employees are not careful, the communication industrialists will be the same untrustworthy, selfish industrialists as the "Robber Barons." The computer executives and stockholders are just as easily given over to greed and desire for power as any other previous industrial moguls. If the industries of the Information Age do not realize their similarities to industries of the past, they will likely meet the same fate as the previous industrialists. In that case, the public will have to create organizations and laws to prevent them from continuing to buy the power, which allows them to ignore the will of the public. If these partnerships between industry and local governments continue without the checks and balances required by our Constitution, self rule will continue to decline.

In the past, liberals or progressives rallied to check the power of the wealthy manufacturers. But at this time, both conservatives and liberals have promoted the decline of majority rule. Many conservatives have always consciously supported using undemocratic practices to promote capitalism. More recently, many modern liberals have entered into the capitalist arena. They have put pressure on capitalists to be more responsive to the needs of the people, but they have not demanded that they be responsive to the will of the people. Liberals have fallen into the arrogant attitude that they know how best to create a just society. In their arrogance, they have now joined the many conservatives who have historically ignored the will of the people. Although having a different motive, modern liberals have been imposing their so-called benevolent will upon the majority. They have become equally responsible for the recent decline in the rule of the people.

Another example of the loss of self-rule locally can be seen in the popularity of initiatives being placed on the ballot by citizen groups in states that allow it. These propositions reflect the frustration of the public with their representatives who are failing to respond to their will. Over the years, the majority has expressed its will by polls and elections, only to be ignored. Then, a group of citizens has put an initiative on the ballot. Once the initiative is passed, state politicians and bureaucrats who have conflicting, political beliefs or loyalties to some special interest resist enforcing the proposition. A strategy is developed by politicians, bureaucrats and opposing special interests to take the proposition to court. It is held in court for years until the citizens forget about it. Finally, some means is found through the courts or through some settlement to nullify the will of the people. Again, representatives or bureaucrats follow their own best interests or what they deem to be the best interest of the people.

These are only a few examples of hundreds or thousands of daily acts in which representatives across the United States ignore the will or form the opinion of the public. These acts are all proof of the many failures in our republican form of government.

The Decline Of Civility

The decline of civility is not too difficult to prove. People complain daily of inconsiderate and uncivilized behavior by children and adults. Manners and mores seem to have fallen to a new low. My daughter tells me that she is constantly having to take her children's toys back from children in the park who just come up and take them without asking. Sometimes, when she goes to the parents to get the toy back, she is given a lecture on teaching her children how to share. She says that many of the children she encounters are being raised by nannies or daycare providers, and they have not been taught manners.

In addition, I find that many of the teenagers I teach in adult education have poor manners. I will go out of my way to help them, and only a few have thanked me. They will be friendly and show some appreciation, but they very rarely say the words, "thank you." Even day-to-day, when I give them some special help, they have not been trained to express appreciation. Sometimes they whisper, "thank you," as they walk away. They seem to feel they deserve to be helped. Often, if I really go out of my way to give them some extra work or arrange a plan to help them graduate, they stop coming soon after, and I never hear from them again. It is as if the help takes away their motivation; they want someone to do it for them. This is a very common attitude with young people because since the 1960s, there has been less of a commitment to teaching good manners. Manners fell out of favor at that time because they were deemed phony; they have not made a complete comeback in our present culture.

These examples are only mild versions of much deeper problems. Road-Rage killings, the repeated acts of violence and then suicide of depressed and vindictive relatives, hate crimes, and most tragically, the many massacres of youth on ghetto streets and at schools across America are examples of the much deeper problems facing Americans. These violent acts reveal the extreme deterioration of civility, which is the demise of the traditional culture of America. "When the continuity of the traditions of civility is ruptured, the community is threatened. Unless the rupture is repaired, the community will break down into factional, class, racial, and regional wars."[4] this prediction by Lippmann has been fulfilled since the 1960s.

In the 1990s, we saw expressions of the rupture of civility. What happened in Littleton, Colorado in April of 1999 and in seven other schools in the United States since October of 1997 were instances of the complete breakdown of the public philosophy and principles of civility. When boys can kill classmates at close range while laughing and joking, we know something very wrong has happened in our society. Obviously, the consciences of Harris and Klebold, the shooters at Columbine High School, were not tuned to a moral standard of right and wrong founded on the natural law or any religious doctrine. They broke the moral law against murder, and they broke every moral principle in a deep and evil manner. If these were isolated instances, we would have no cause to worry. But they are becoming the norm not the exception.

More On The Ideas Of The Founding Fathers

As mentioned earlier, the public philosophy for America was derived from the culmination of Enlightenment and Judeo-Christian ideas in the minds of our Founding Fathers in the eighteenth century. Natural law and Christian ideas were thoroughly intertwined, even in those founders who were not Christians. In this section, I am going to concentrate on the ideas influenced by Enlightenment thinking. I will bring in the religious elements only when needed to express the flavor of American thought reaching back to its Puritan heritage. Later, I will define those ideas unique to the Puritan belief system.

Most of the Founding Fathers, because of Puritan influence, were not as positive about the goodness and perfectibility of human nature as were some of the European Enlightenment philosophers such as Locke, Montesquieu, or Voltaire. Madison illustrated his thoughts on human nature when he wrote "But what is government itself but the greatest of all reflections on human nature?" The kind of government and the devices of government are determined by the makeup of human nature. He went on to explain: "If men were angels, no government would be necessary…In framing a government which is to be administered by men over men, the great difficulty lies in this, you must first enable the government to control the governed; and in the next place oblige it to control itself."[5] Madison expressed the commonly held belief of the Founding Fathers about human nature. Their perception of it was the chief influence on the formation of the public philosophy. Citizens at that time agreed that you could not trust humans to do what was right from natural inclinations, especially when it came to ruling. They did not believe, as did Rousseau, an eighteenth century French philosopher, that natural man was more perfect than civilized man.

The founders believed that man-in-the-state-of-nature, without civilizing traditions, would act from his lower, instinctual nature and not from reason. Jefferson stated critically that "the numbers of men in all ages have preferred ease, slumber, and good cheer to liberty, when they have been in competition. We must not then depend alone upon the love of liberty in the soul of man for its preservation."[6] To succeed in creating the good society, citizens needed to read any book which "contributes to fix us in the principles and practice the art of virtue…dispositions of the mind, like limbs of the body, acquire strength by exercise. But exercise produces habit; and in the instance of which we speak, the exercise being of the moral feelings, produces a habit of thinking and acting virtuously."[7] For a person to possess virtue meant he would act and think rightly and possess moral goodness. Colonial citizens were of two minds about virtue: one believed pleasing God was the end of man, and he would achieve his goal by seeking virtue. The others believed happiness was the end of man, but a person could not achieve happiness without obtaining virtue. Although having different goals, early American citizens agreed that seeking virtue was the path to fulfill their goal. In that belief they were united.

Benjamin Franklin was a great enthusiast for developing virtue. He wrote and spoke about the industrious virtues that have been a part of all immigrants who came to this country. He extolled hard work, good use of time, moderation, and common sense. At one point in his life he decided he wanted to obtain moral perfection. He set out to acquire all moral virtues. He put himself on a weekly program; he "determined to give a week's strict attention to each of the virtues successively."[8] He had a list of thirteen virtues: temperance, silence, order, resolution, frugality, industry, sincerity, justice, moderation, cleanliness, tranquillity, chastity, and humility. As did Jefferson, he saw acquiring virtue as an art: "Most people have naturally some virtues, but none have naturally all the virtues. To acquire those that are wanting and secure what we acquire, as well as those we have naturally, is the subject of an art."[9]

The Founding Father's emphasis on virtue was a means to check the excesses of human nature. However, they did not believe principles defining right behavior and traditions of civility were to be found only in Christian doctrines or the teachings of religion. They firmly believed these moral principles could also be found in natural laws. Lippmann warned not to confuse natural laws with scientific laws. He insisted, "They do not describe human behavior as it is. They prescribe what it should be. They do not predict what men will actually do. They are principles of right behavior in the good society governed by the western traditions of civility."[10] The goals of the Founding Fathers were to maintain the practice of the principles of right behavior found in religion and natural law and then establish a republican government of checks and balances to protect against the weaknesses of human nature.

Besides the virtues or principles of the public philosophy already mentioned, there were others that were directly connected to societal relationships. These defined the duties of property not just its rights. They provided the goal of free speech to discover truth, and ascertained that the use of deception was a violation of those principles. They confirmed that "there is a rational order of things in which it is possible, by sincere inquiry and rational debate to distinguish the true and the false, the right and the wrong, the good which leads to the realization of the human ends and the evil which leads to the destruction and death of civility."[11] The Founding Fathers based and built our form of government on the expectation and necessity that the United States would continuously live and be governed by the public philosophy. They feared the loss of principle and virtue would condemn their glorious experiment to failure.

Lippmann agreed with the Founding Fathers because he saw that the fabric of civil society and community were dependent on the public philosophy. He knew that when citizens lose the rules of civility and the principles of conduct, all areas of a society deteriorate. In his view "In the maintenance and formation of a true community the articulate philosophy is, one might say, like the thread which holds the pieces of the fabric together. Not everyone can have mastered the philosophy; most people, presumably, may have heard almost nothing about it. But if among the people of light and leading the public philosophy has, as the Chinese say, the Mandate of Heaven, the beliefs and the habits which cause men to collaborate will remain whole. But if the public philosophy is discarded, being treated as reactionary or nonsensical; then the stitches will have been pulled out and the fabric will come apart."[12]

Why The Fabric Of Society Has Come Apart

The fabric of society comes apart when there is no public philosophy because, without traditions of civility, people yield to their lower nature and are unable to unite into a society. There are two parts to human nature: he higher nature and the lower nature. The higher attributes of human nature are the part of mankind that gives them their humanity in contrast to being animalistic. The higher nature is attracted to love, self-control, dignity, duty, self-sacrifice, learning, and forgiveness. The citizens in a society with traditions of civility are encouraged to strive to attain high, moral and civil goals. They are encouraged to cultivate high, moral character. The desire to be good residing in the higher nature is inspired to the highest human potential for goodness by the goals of the public philosophy.

The lower attributes of human nature are more akin to the instinctual aspects of animal nature. On the positive side, they provide humans with warmth, emotional responses, earthy feelings, and sexual impulses. Without the lower nature, humans can be distant and rigid. However, if the lower nature rules people, it causes them to follow their instincts, desires, impulses and emotions without the use of reason. They will lack self-control and can easily yield to the negative emotions of hatred, rage and revenge. The 1960s and 70s motto, "if it feels good, do it," makes an appeal to the lower nature. People who follow this motto have less self-discipline and less ability to sacrifice for others. They do whatever gives them pleasure. They exhibit little self-control in sexuality, drugs, alcohol, food, or other sense-driven areas. Moreover, those controlled by the lower nature are often attracted to money and power. These two areas of desire cause the most animalistic behavior. (The lower nature is not evil; it just needs to be controlled by the higher nature.)

To preserve civility, the standards of the public philosophy must be high; in fact, according to natural law principles, they must be unreachable. A student of human nature knows that the lower nature of humans makes most people lazy and mediocre. In school, the majority of students are satisfied to be average. Only a few desire excellence. If students are presented with a very high standard—expected to learn difficult subject matter—those who are ambitious will manage to learn almost all that is presented to them. The average student, while obtaining less knowledge, will still acquire considerable knowledge because they have had to work hard to make a "C" grade. If the standards in schools are low and the students are not expected to learn difficult subject matter, the ambitious will still reach or nearly reach the highest standard, although learning less, but the majority will only seek to achieve a "C" grade. Therefore, they will learn very little. Consequently, schools need to appeal to the higher nature of students and expect them to learn difficult subject matter.

In like manner, principles of conduct must be set very high. In fact, these standards must be unreachable in order to motivate the majority of people (who accept being average) to exert themselves sufficiently to make them fully civilized. Although character standards should be out of reach, they should not be inordinately beyond reach. Unrealistic standards cause discouragement. At the same time, ethical standards must not be set low. If they are, the lower nature will cause behavior to fall considerably beneath what is considered acceptable in a society. A society needs to instruct its people to endeavor to achieve the most excellent virtues; then its people will manifest a greater capacity to love and less of a tendency to be self-absorbed. Citizens need to understand that the traditions of civility are an ideal to which they commit their greatest effort, always knowing that they will never truly achieve the ideal. It is their constant striving to achieve the ideal that will make them people of good character. Anything less than a high standard will result in disruptive, uncivilized behavior.

We have in this country today many examples of how lowered standards have produced lawless behavior. For example, sometime during the 1970s, a decision was made to remove the standard of love towards our neighbor and replace it with tolerance. Tolerance has been a byword for the liberal movement. We must all be tolerant of different cultures and races. By lowering the standard, the lower nature has had more influence on behavior than the higher nature; and as the years have passed, there has been less tolerance. There is especially less tolerance by liberals of anyone who disagrees with their politically correct terminology. The consequence of lowering the standard from love to tolerance can be clarified by using an analogy: My husband and I have a dog, Lucky, and a cat, Twerp. Lucky and Twerp tolerate each other. When Lucky comes into Twerp's room, my office, he begins to scratch himself near her bed, acting as if she were not there. He scratches the metal tags on his collar, making a loud jangling sound. Twerp always tenses up when she hears that sound. Then, she starts to lick herself, likewise pretending she does not see him. They play a passive game, pretending they are not bothered about each other's presence.

However, if Lucky comes up behind Twerp, and she does not see him, he will jump at her and try to bite her. If Lucky gets too close to Twerp's bed, she hisses at him and raises her back. When Lucky is not in his room, sometimes Twerp will go into his room, our bedroom, and jump up into Lucky's chair. One day Lucky found her in his bed—pandemonium followed. Twerp jumped wildly past Lucky, sprinting down the hall with him right behind her. She was out the dog/cat door and down the street in a matter of seconds. Lucky stayed right behind her until she jumped over a fence. Obviously, Lucky and Twerp have the ability to tolerate each other, but their tolerance is fragile. If they see an opportunity, they will undermine, attack, and try to dominate.

If Lucky and Twerp had affection for each other, their relationship would be more peaceful. With affection, they could trust each other. Then, they could turn their backs without fear. So too, humans must have more than tolerance to secure peace. The multicultural groups in the United States can only have peace when they are called upon to love each other. When people are told they are obligated to love and respect their neighbor, not just tolerate them, they develop a greater capacity to accept each other. The majority may not achieve the goal of love; but as a result of reaching for the higher goal, they will acquire a much greater level of acceptance and respect, thereby, producing accord.

Lucky and Twerp, being a dog and cat, show animal behavior by having natural enmity. Human nature has a lower part that is more like animals. If we set our standards too low, our lower nature rules and the threads of the social fabric spoken of by Lippmann are broken. If we are told to tolerate each other instead of to love each other, we cannot even tolerate each other. We fail to tolerate each other because the majority is willing to put only mediocre effort into achieving tolerance. Therefore, they will fall short of tolerance and fall into dissension and division. Some animals can learn to have affection for those of other species. How much more capable are humans than animals to create unity out of a diverse society since they are of the same species and have the ability to rationally choose to love others.

Summary

In summary, the public philosophy was a set of principles derived through religion, reason, and natural laws that created a society motivated to achieve the common good through the decisions of its government and the civility of its citizens. It considered and protected the rights of its citizens. But it was equally, if not more, set upon requiring its citizens to fulfill their duties and responsibilities to their neighbors and their communities. The traditional laws of civility were universal and absolute. They were based upon the Golden Rule—to do unto others as you would want them to do unto you and the Christian law of love—to love your neighbor as yourself. Other members of the community were seen as more important than oneself, and personal sacrifice was expected for the good of the whole community. The public philosophy, because it was based on unselfish service, restrained the animal, selfish, instinctual aspects of human nature. It provided the manners, norms, and values that made individuals trustworthy, responsible, courageous, honest, upright, respectful, and forgiving. These are the kinds of individuals or citizens on which the Founding Fathers depended to make their democratic, republican Constitution work.

A general dissolution of principles and manners will more surely overthrow the liberties of America more than the whole force of the common enemy. While the people remain virtuous they cannot be subdued; but when once they lose their virtue they will be ready to surrender their liberties to the first external or internal invader. How necessary is it for those who are determined to transmit the blessing of liberty as a fair inheritance to posterity to associate on the public principles in support of public virtue...If virtue and knowledge are diffused among the people, they will never be enslaved. This will be their great security. Virtue and knowledge will forever be an even balance for powers and riches. I hope our countrymen will never depart from the principles and maxims that have been handed down to us from our wise forefathers. This greatly depends upon the example of men of character and influence of the present day.[13]

What Is The Modern Philosophy?

Now we will compare the modern, popular philosophy which guides and directs the lives of Americans today to the public philosophy that was the guide for civilized, public behavior up until the end of the nineteenth century, and, to some degree, up until the 1960s. The thought of our present philosophy in comparison to the earlier one makes me feel embarrassed to even begin. There is such a notable contrast between our present shallow, self-centered culture and values and the unselfish, duty-based culture and values of previous generations of Americans.

The America of today is not the child of the 1960s; it is the child of the Industrial Revolution and the suicide of traditional liberalism in the 1960s. The Industrial Age, which began at the end of the nineteenth century, introduced new ideas and practices which undermined the public philosophy. The scientific-based industrial philosophies—laissez faire, the survival of the fittest (Darwinism), Utilitarian, and individualism—attacked the public philosophy. They glorified ideas and goals, which were the opposite of the traditional rules of civility for the good of society. They began to question the ability of any moral code to be based on universal principles of right and wrong found in natural laws. Later, in the twentieth century, the industrial philosophies added the scientific theory of relativity to their collection. This scientific theory was falsely applied to ethics, stating that ethics were relative and situational.

The purpose of the industrial philosophies was to win public favor for the free market capitalism that was on the rise. Elements of the public philosophy resisted the goals of industrialists. It censored self-interest and greed. The rules of civility taught that individuals should seek to become rich, not for one's own gain, but so that one could benefit the community. The traditional values placed a duty on all institutions of society, including business or property, to care for the poor and weak. However, capitalists wanted freedom from duties to society. They espoused the philosophy of the survival of the fittest: Those who were fit to make money survived and prospered; those who were weak worked for the capitalists. Excessive work was the lot of the less fit who would die off to make room for evolution of the fittest. Moreover, they created a "laissez faire" philosophy to support free economic activity without regulations and controls.

Walter Lippmann maintained that "In the prevailing popular culture of the West all philosophies are the instruments of some man's purpose, all truths are self-centered and self-regarding, and all principles are the rationalizations of some special interest."[14]

Capitalists continued to gain excessive power and influence by undermining the public philosophy that had guided property relationships during the seventeenth and eighteenth centuries. In these traditions, private property did not have absolute rights and "despotic dominion." There were duties and responsibilities associated with private property. Nineteenth century philosophers "broke with the public philosophy and the traditions of civility...For a time they excluded from political philosophy, from jurisprudence, and from legislation almost any notion that property had duties as well as rights."[15] During the Industrial Revolution what was known as the property class was now reinterpreted to mean massive corporations possessing the means of employment and survival for millions. The traditional values that had always laid duties and responsibilities on the propertied class no longer existed. This shift in philosophy and law enabled corporations then and now to expand their power and unite with other factions to establish their control of society.

The Republican Party and the Modern Philosophy:

The Republican Party, which was formed before the Civil War, became the bearer of the public philosophy whose principles supported the preservation of the Union and the abolishment of slavery. Abraham Lincoln, more than the party, was a man of conscience; he stamped his character on the party. But after his death, the conservative civil values suffered from the rise to power of wealthy industrialists. (In this book the highest form of conservatism will be called, civil conservatism, in contrast to the economic conservatism that proceeded from the Industrial Revolution.) After the War, the Republican Party carried the burden of preserving civil conservatism. This conservatism was supposed to be a harmonious combination of the traditions of civility for social (public), political, private (personal), and economic conduct. In this political philosophy, private property had duties to society, and there were restrictions on the power of economic forces in order to protect and promote individual rights.

As we have seen, the industrial philosophy or economic conservatism promoted self-interest, less government, fewer regulations, and the self-made man. This economic conservatism slowly outweighed and nullified civil conservatism. Somehow the Republican intellectuals and politicians of the late nineteenth and twentieth centuries lost sight of the responsibility of conservative thinking. They had been enticed into the camp of the capitalists. The Republican Party increasingly became the party of economic, not civil, conservatism.

The Republicans Miss The Mark:

By the 1960s, the Republican Party had mixed many of the New Deal ideas into their political philosophy. Because of the problems of the depression of the 1930s, they had yielded to using government for public benefit. However, they were still the party of big business, and they had not reintroduced the public philosophy back into America's consciousness. Surprisingly, the politician to most closely espouse civil conservatism in the 1960s was a Democrat, John F. Kennedy. Kennedy defined his version of the public philosophy in his book, *Profiles In Courage,* published in 1956.

In 1960, Republican Senator Barry Goldwater came forward to define what he called, *The Conscience of the Conservative.* This book on conservatism did not restore the civil traditions or public philosophy to the Republican Party. Instead, he clarified the industrial, economic philosophy that had been watered down during the New Deal. He described the old mixture of less government, less taxes, and more individual self-determination. Goldwater added a spiritual aspect to economics. He maintained that "the Conservative has learned that the economic and spiritual aspects of man's nature are inextricably intertwined."[16] He was warning people against individuals depending on the state and losing their spiritual freedom. But he did not describe the weakened state of the individual standing alone against big business. His assertion strengthened economic conservatism. His theory helped to reestablish the power of the capitalist elite in government circles. He drew people back to the economic, self-interest conservatism that was contrary to the thinking of the Founding Fathers who never separated the values of unselfish public service and character building from economic values.

Summary of the Economic Conservative Influence

By the 1960s, through the use of the media, especially with the massive influence of television in the 1950s, the public had accepted the self-interest, materialistic values fed to them by industrialists. The Republican Party continued to be representative of big business and the economic conservatism that was associated with the industrial philosophy. The presidency of Dwight D. Eisenhower during most of the 1950s presided over self-satisfied, materialist American citizens enjoying the height of prosperity in the Industrial Age. The public had become less concerned with duties and righting injustices and concentrated, instead, on increased desires for consumer goods and enjoying the good life. To them the pursuit of happiness did not mean the pursuit of virtue; it meant pursuing material possessions and increasing leisure pleasures. Of course, as we will see, the children of these fifties' parents were not as content or compliant.

The Liberals Fight Back

Unpredictably, the 1960s and the 1970s unleashed revolutionary, liberal values that challenged the complacency of Americans and their industrial values. There was a promising interlude during the presidency of John F. Kennedy and the civil rights activities of Martin Luther King, Jr. that will be described in the next chapter. In this chapter, we are seeking to understand the elements of the modern philosophy of the present society. We have seen the move of Americans away from the traditional values of virtue and duty to the industrial values of self-interest, materialism, and consumerism. Then, in the 1960s, the liberal left, reacting against the industrial values, introduced new values into the mix. Sadly, these liberal values of the 1960s and 1970s were the final act of philosophical violence that killed the public philosophy.

The liberal left of the 1970s was probably unaware of their participation in the death of the philosophy that could have saved the republic. In their frustration with the industrial ideas and the "military industrial complex," which was undermining American democracy, they mistakenly identified it with the traditions of civility or the best of western civilization provided by the public philosophy. They recognized one conservative philosophy when there were actually two—economic conservatism (capitalism) and civil conservatism (the public philosophy). Liberals were either ignorant of or ignored the public philosophy because they introduced a new philosophy into the American consciousness to combat the capitalist ideas. I call this liberal philosophy the man-in-the-state-of-nature or natural-is-good philosophy (not the same as a belief in natural laws).

Liberal philosophy was anti-capitalist and anti-civilization. Sixties' activists erroneously sought to overthrow the traditions of civility in their efforts to correct some valid, societal injustices. They mistakenly identified civil conservatism with economic conservatism; therefore they overthrew all conservative traditions. They were unaware that without civil conservatism society falls into a state of nature where animal-type instincts rule rather than the rule of law and the rule of universal moral standards.

The Modern Philosophy

From the late 1960s onward, we can describe the modern philosophy of our society as a combination of industrial, now corporate, and liberal values (natural-is-good). The liberal values were transferred to the people by the same methods of manipulation and deception as had been used and continue to be used by the industrialists or corporations. Liberals also seductively used the media to further conform the culture to their values. Through all of their efforts, they have not succeeded in removing any of the influence of the corporate or industrial philosophies; instead, they have added to that culture of self-interest and materialism their own brand of selfishness and narcissism.

From the liberal left, the public learned about self-love, self-importance, self-esteem, and self-absorption. They were told that possessing happiness was the right of every citizen. Because suffering was an enemy of happiness, it could no longer have the redeeming value of building good character. All people deserved to be happy, and if someone or something prevented their happiness, they had a right to fight against them, using moral or immoral means. Americans were told that every individual had the right to decide his or her own right and wrong. Ethics were relative to every situation, and a person should be guided in moral issues by how they felt at the moment. As a result of this liberal philosophy, today's America consists of many individuals seeking their own self-fulfillment to the neglect of their children, neighbors, communities, and nation.

There has been some modification of the earlier hedonistic beliefs of the 1960s and 1970s that insisted "if it feels good, do it," and that each person should "do their own thing." The public has moderated some of its excesses. When the Aids epidemic came into the sexual picture, many Americans moderated their sexual activities. Moreover, during the nineties, the public had moments of awareness that something was wrong in our country. Periodically, citizens complained that Americans had become self-centered and greedy, but they felt powerless to change the national character.

Americans question the direction of our country every time we have a mass killing, especially if the massacre involves middle-class children. When the two boys at Columbine High School killed and wounded classmates without appearing to have any conscience, it momentarily stirred the public to once more question what was wrong with our nation. The leaders told them it was the guns; and again, people immediately calmed down, welcoming an answer to distract them from the truth. Of course, this is a state of denial that pacifies people. It keeps them from seeing that the true problem is the loss of the traditions of civility or the public philosophy.

The modern philosophy, although recently modified, still could not be more opposed to the public philosophy. Our forefathers placed virtue and good character as the highest aim of mankind while the modern philosophy puts self-fulfillment and happiness as its highest aim. The traditions of civility had people live by the Golden Rule and put the interests of others and one's country before their own interests. The modern philosophy places self-interest and self-love before family, neighbors, or country. It puts rights before duties, self-gratification before responsibilities, and possessions before relationships. These priorities prevent people from being responsible citizens—intelligently ruling by expressing their well-informed opinions to their representatives. Moreover, self-centeredness and materialism interfere with the public formulating the best decisions for the common good.

In the next chapter, we will learn the crucial importance of the message and vision of John F. Kennedy for America. We will discover how, when Kennedy died, his vision became dormant and his effort to restore the public philosophy was left uncultivated. Moreover, we will understand how the death of John F. Kennedy, and to a lesser degree Martin Luther King, Jr. and Bobby Kennedy, caused the traditional liberal movement to self-destruct. It will become clear how the new liberal agenda increased the hold of the power elite—the "military industrial complex" or "The Establishment"—by increasing the demise of the traditions of civility that are needed to guarantee republican government and a civilized culture.

Chapter 2.

Kennedy's Death Unleashes Liberal Excesses

The Republican Form Of Government

Before we study the role of Kennedy in the demise of our culture and the weakening of our republic, we need to understand the ideas that guided the Founding Fathers in the creation of the American republic. By knowing their ideas, we can measure our present system of government by that ideal standard. Then we will know if not only our culture has changed but also our government. Through the Constitution, the Founding Fathers set up a very complex republican form of government. They created and depended upon multiple checks and balances to protect the common good.

Let us review the initial republican system developed by the Founding Fathers. Our system of government consists of a complex set of checks and balances. It is founded on a belief that society can be protected from flawed motives by creating a government with "opposite and rival interests."

The Founding Fathers put great thought into creating a government in which an aristocracy, an individual, or the majority could not obtain absolute power. As mentioned in Chapter One, the founders knew that "If men were angels, no government would be necessary…In framing a government which is to be administered by men over men, the great difficulty lies in this: you must first enable the government to control the governed; and in the next place oblige it to control itself."[1] To help the government control itself, Madison explains that the "constant aim is to divide and arrange the several offices in such a manner as that each is a check on the other—that the private interest of every individual may be a sentinel over the public rights."[2]

Three separate branches of government were created at the federal level to act as a check on each other—the Congressional, Executive, and Judicial Branches. Moreover, a federal system was created to assure the rights and powers of individual colonies or states, which therefore limited the power of the federal government. In order to limit the power of the majority from oppressing the minority and to assure the majority would promote the common good, they trusted in the diversity of social factions. They saw the distinctions between different interests as a safeguard for democracy. "In all civilized Societies, distinctions are various and unavoidable...there will be rich and poor; creditors and debtors; a landed interest, a monied interest, a mercantile interest, a manufacturing interest. These classes may again be subdivided..." The Founding Fathers believed the people were the only safe depositors of power as long as multiple factions kept them from uniting through a common interest and thereby abuse the minority. "If then there must be different interests and parties in Society; and a majority when united by a common interest or passion cannot be restrained from oppressing the minority, what remedy can be found in a republican Government, where the majority must ultimately decide, but that of giving such an extent to its sphere, that no common interest or passion will be likely to unite a majority of the whole number in an unjust pursuit."[3] He expressed the same idea further on in Federalist Paper 51, by stating that the federal republic of the United States "Whilst all authority in it will be derived from and dependent on the society, the society itself will be broken into many parts, interests and classes of citizens, that the rights of individuals, or of the minority, will be in little danger from interested combinations of the majority."[4]

Madison reasoned that multiple factions could seldom unite into a majority to oppress the minority or pursue an unjust cause. The majority would choose the common good because the conflicting factions would have to consider all the various interests in order to reach a compromise. It would be unlikely, he stated, for a coalition to form on any "other principles than those of justice and the general good." This would be especially true in a larger society, like the United States, with a greater number of factions, than in the smaller local and state societies. The smaller societies would be more vulnerable to civil injustices than would happen in the larger federal society.

Madison saw "justice as the end of government. It is the end of civil society." He and the other Founding Fathers depended upon this theory of competing factions to preserve the republic from a few factions uniting to acquire majority support and thereby, oppress the weaker factions or the minority. If a stronger faction formed and united a majority of the whole society, the society would fall into anarchy similar to the state of nature. The minority who was denied their rights would rise up against the majority causing anarchy. Madison's hope was that once anarchy reigned, the stronger faction would out of this anarchy call for a government to be formed to protect all of its citizens, establishing a government ruled by "a will independent of the society itself."[5] Madison and the other founders saw government as beholden, not to the will of the majority or a minority, but to the general good.

The most recent and clearest example of the process in which a few factions united and gained majority support was the Vietnam War. Congress never declared war against Vietnam. It was an Executive war, reaching its full fury under the presidency of Lyndon B. Johnson. The military, government, and defense industry united in their purposes. Their purposes were ideological and financial. This coalition of factions moved the United States into war without much resistance by the majority. Since the war progressed gradually and without a debate or declaration of war by the Congress, the majority of citizens did not question it. Then, slowly, opposition to the war grew. Many of the recently college-educated youth began to question its validity. Increasingly, the opposition took to the streets. Dissension escalated until, at the Democratic Convention in 1968 in Chicago, anarchy reigned. Americans watched police brutally beat some of their own children on television. Moreover, during the same period, anarchy and dissatisfaction was expressed by blacks in the ghettos with the death of King Consequently, as opposition to the war expanded, an increasing number of Americans began to object to the war. Finally, the military, government, and defense industry responded to anarchy by seeking the common good of the whole society. Even before the Chicago Convention, Johnson, a Democrat, refused to run for another term of office; and Richard Nixon, a Republican, won the presidency, promising to end the war.

The era of the 1960s should have been a warning to factions or special interests in our country not to unite for personal gain. That era was living proof that the Founding Fathers were right: rival factions are needed to provide justice for all individuals in society. The common good can only be obtained in a democratic republic by constant friction between factions, without a few special interests uniting by compromising their principles in order to gain majority support.

Madison was wrong about the ability of factions to unite in a country as large as the United States. He could not predict the advent of the media and psychology. Unfortunately, special interests did not learn the right lessons from the 1960s. Special interests have only become more insidious in their methods and increased the number of groups who have adopted those methods. Both liberal groups and economic conservatives are working to achieve their goals through interlocking interests uniting for their various objectives.

Some Adjustments To The Theory Of Factions

After the American system of government had been functioning for a few years, some modifications developed having to do with factions.

Most of the founders had hoped they could avoid establishing the entrenched parties existing in England. They saw parties and political compromise as corrupting to their idealistic experiment. To their grief, parties and political haggling could not be avoided. A complete "free market" competition of factions was unworkable. Without the union of various special interests, nothing could be accomplished.

Parties became the means to limit competition in government in order to reach agreements and pass laws. Unregulated competition in government was just as destructive as unregulated competition in the free market. In government, as in economics, passions and competition run out of control, leading to the use of dishonest methods to achieve one's ends. Individual forces, in order to obtain power and promote their individual agendas, will use any means to win. The idea of the survival of the fittest leads to anarchy and finally, one winner. Therefore, the idea of factions expressed by Madison was modified by the party system. Politicians had to learn to compromise and unite various interests under different parties in order for compromise to be achieved and the republican idea to work. On the other hand, the early parties did not unite factions in such a way as to create complete agreement at all times with those factions in each party. There were constant shifts of loyalty and different unions of special interests, allowing for power shifts in the parties. In this way no one group or small group of special interests monopolized all of the power.

Again, the capitalist model is a good analogy. When one corporation determines to limit all competition by buying up other corporations in its same domain, then they can set prices and gauge the consumers. So, also, political groups must not unite with complete agreement in all areas. When special interests concede principle in the process of making concessions, they are selling out the public good for the sake of power. When the Executive or Congressional Branches unite with industry in order to gain financial support for the party or for a worthy program, they are leaving principle behind. The public did not elect corporations; it elected those in government. It is wrong for government to hand power over to corporations for the sake of gaining political power or accomplishing a worthy goal. In other words, the Department of Commerce can protect and promote American financial interests, but it should not arrange for the contact between specific corporations and foreign governmental and financial institutions. The laissez-faire approach to global capitalism is politically unethical in a republican democracy. It violates the principles of the check and balance system by "rival factions" depended upon by our Founding Fathers to preserve our form of government.

There are numerous examples of unethical unions between business and government. Here are two that have been publicized in the last year. First, the special favors given to Loreal by the Executive Branch to supply satellite, technological know-how to the Chinese went too far and led to compromising American missile technology. Second, when the Clinton administration hired John Huang to work in the Commerce Department, all along knowing of his Chinese connections, it crossed an ethical line. At the Commerce Department, Huang was involved in international economic policy at the same time he kept in contact with the Riadys, who had holdings in the Lippo Group's world banking operation. These are examples of common practices, supported by both parties, which have developed over the last twenty years. They show how boundaries between special interests and government are dissolving. As our founders understood, too much unity can weaken republican government.

As mentioned earlier, there has to be some unification of special interests in government to achieve legitimate compromises for the general good of the country. However, special interests and the parties that contain them must limit their compromising practices by principle. As long as factions and party members continue to live by principle, a monopoly of interest cannot be formed. The feminists, a special interest group in the Democratic Party, joined with labor, gays, people of color, environmentalists, and teachers on many issues. They had an opportunity to follow principle in the Clinton/Lewinsky scandal. Beginning with Paula Jones, information continued to pour out showing the misogynist behavior of Clinton. Feminist organizations could have used these examples of misogynist behavior to educate and advance the thinking of men and women on how male-female relationships can be improved. Rather than follow principle, most feminists remained loyal to Clinton and the party line. If they had broken with the party, they would have acted with integrity and with the kind of behavior in keeping with republican principles.

Factions need to live by principle just as much as individuals. If they retain integrity, they will not unite with other special interests to form a political monopoly. Their standards will limit the degree to which they can join with other groups. The principles and goals of each special interest will maintain a healthy competition and check and balance of each faction on all of the others.

Using parties to unite factions has worked over the last two hundred years because a sufficient number of factions and individuals within the parties put principle before self-interest. The majority of special interests and politicians did not practice the philosophy of "the end justifies the means." However, since the loss of the public philosophy, we have seen those in government creating monopolies of special interest instead of practicing non-partisan concessions. Many special interests feel passionately that their goals are of such importance that they are willing to leave principle behind in order to achieve their "virtuous" end. In the process, they are being unfaithful and disloyal to the republican government they should be trying to preserve.

Is The American Republic Still A Republic?

The goals and principles of the Founding Fathers are the standard by which our government and society need to be measured. Let us look at the aspect of rival factions. Does our society still consist of rival interests or are there coalitions of interests oppressing the minority and ignoring the common good? That question is complex and requires some historical review. The Industrial Revolution introduced a union between industry and government, which continues to this day. As a consequence of the Industrial Revolution, industry's influence over government was flagrant and conscious. The early twentieth century was filled with weaker interests struggling against the giants of industry. The corporate heads were continually using their money and power to win favor from politicians. Progressives, Populists, and Labor identified the coalition of government and industry and fought against it. They brought in reforms by using the political process to make representatives more responsive to the majority; i.e., primaries and direct elections of U.S. Senators. Their purposes were not satisfactorily accomplished until the New Deal. Then, because of the extensive poverty caused by the Great Depression, changes were made to protect and provide for lower and middle class Americans.

Although the government under Roosevelt and the New Deal disrupted the power of industry, the corporations reasserted themselves after World War II. The reforms introduced to weaken corporate or business power in the Industrial Age were not sufficient to prevent new alliances in the Information Age. By the 1950s the media inventions of the Information Age—radio, television, and movies—as well as psychological techniques, began to be effectively used to promote consumerism and corporate goals. By the end of the 1950s, as he left office, President Eisenhower warned the nation of the "military-industrial complex." His warning was especially alarming since he had previously been a part of the military as a general. He was exposing a union between industry, the military, and government mentioned above. It was a threat to our democratic, republican form of government.

This coalition consisted of corporate heads, government officials, and military officers intermingling socially and on boards, agencies, and commissions that crisscrossed into all three spheres of influence. C. Wright Mills' classic, *The Power Elite*, written in 1956, gave substantial insight into the coalition between powerful factions, which had evolved over the last century and continue to this day. He stated that: "By the power elite, we refer to those political, economic, and military circles which as an intricate set of overlapping cliques share decisions having at least national consequences. In so far as national events are decided, the power elite are those who decide them."[6] He does not contend that all historical events are determined by this elite; he does contend that, depending on their reach of power, they do determine most major historical occurrences, such as many wars, political elections, and foreign policy decisions. "The minimum definition of the power elite as those who decide whatever is decided of major consequence, does not imply that the members of this elite are always and necessarily the history-makers; neither does it imply that they never are."[7]

Returning to the ideas of the Founding Fathers about the danger of coalitions creating strong factions, we can see that they were right. The uniting of government and large industries in the Industrial Age undermined our republic. These two factions enticed support from the majority, thereby oppressing the minority of small farmers, businesses, and laborers. They achieved their goals by using faulty philosophies which encouraged the value of self-interest, extolling the survival of the fittest (those who are the rich or middle class), and promoting the theory of laissez-faire—an idea that protected monopolies and trusts from regulations and limitations. In 1955, Lippmann already decried the state of American politics and society. He and C. Wright Mills both saw the beginnings, or to them the extensively impaired state, of American society and its republican government.

As we have seen, Lippmann placed the responsibility for the decline of democracy and western society upon the fact that Americans "are cut off from the public philosophy and the political arts which are needed to govern the liberal democratic society...They are the principles of right behavior in the good society governed by the western traditions of civility."[8] He saw the public philosophy being replaced by the self-interest, industrial philosophies promoted by economic conservatives and new liberal ideas. C. Wright Mills blamed the deterioration of the republic on the union of powerful factions, a power elite—a group of insiders consisting of economic conservatives— who were changing the traditional views of Americans and asserting political power at will.

My purpose in this book is not to prove there is a power elite. I am mentioning this age-old phenomenon in order explain the elements leading up to the revolution that occurred in the 1960s and 1970s. As we have seen the new propertied class, the industrialists failed in their responsibilities to society during the Industrial Revolution. They used faulty philosophy to obtain majority support. It took the activism of small farmers, small businesses, and the laboring class with the final horrendous depression of the 1930s to dislodge some of the corporate power. From World War II onward industry or corporations instituted another surge of influence by combining with the military and government, using the power of the media to subdue and win over the majority.

Use Of The Media By The Power Elite

The "military-industrial complex" or "The Establishment" as it was referred to by the liberals of the 1960s developed techniques of manipulation using the media. The public consists of individuals with certain learned knowledge and first-hand experience. When the public depends upon the media for its information, its knowledge and experience become determined by the media. As the twentieth century progressed, the elite or economic conservatives, many of whom were and are part of the media, developed stereotypes to filter information to the public. Public debate began to wither as the media not only reported but also interpreted information. There was little room for feedback by the public. Mills contended that the public of the fifties had been turned into the masses. The forming of public opinion protected the elite from the public by turning them into a mass. "With the broadening of the base of politics within the context of a folk-lore of democratic decision-making, and with the increased means of mass persuasion that are available, the public of public opinion has become the object of intensive efforts to control, manage, manipulate, and increasingly intimidate."9

The political, military and economic coalition of the 1950s used the media and knowledge of psychology to guide public experience and opinion. The fears of our Founding Fathers had been realized when the powerful factions of government, military and corporations united and began to psychologically manage the public. Gouverneur Morris, at the Constitutional Convention, declared his fears of the ability of the rich to seduce and confuse the masses. He described his fears when he declared: "Let the rich mix with the poor in a Commercial Country, they will establish an oligarchy (rule of the few). Take away commerce, and the democracy will triumph..." The influence of the rich is to be feared because "the people never act from reason alone. The Rich will take advantage of their passions & make these the instruments for oppressing them...The schemes of the Rich will be favored by the extent of the Country...They (the people) will be the dupes of those who have more knowledge and intercourse."10

The Response Of Liberals
To The Elite In The 1960s

It is at this point in time, in the 1960s, that one of the greatest tragedies occurred in the twentieth century. It is a tragedy with far-reaching consequences—hopefully reversible. With the election of John F. Kennedy, Democrats felt new hope for justice and the liberal causes. Kennedy was defining a path that would have strengthened our republican form of government. He was not challenging economic conservatives directly. His political philosophy was an indirect challenge. By calling the masses back to unselfish public service, he was awakening in the people a feeling of hope to regain control of their lives, their society, and their government. He was calling them back from being the masses into becoming again, the public. Americans elected Kennedy because they unconsciously knew that something was wrong with the society and the country. They did not know what was wrong, but they felt Kennedy had the right answers.

When President Kennedy came to office, he not only called the people back to unselfish behavior. What he was really doing was calling Americans back to some of the elements of the public philosophy that Lippmann believed could restore the traditions of our society and our traditional form of government. Whether consciously or unconsciously, Kennedy was trying to revive the public philosophy. He came into office with a personal commitment to the traditions of civility. He was a traditional liberal (a Jefferson liberal); not a part of the liberal left that came into power after his death. In his book, *Profiles In Courage,* he illuminated the values and principles of that public philosophy. He introduced the readers to senators who had been willing to sacrifice their positions, reputations, and power in order to follow their consciences and choose the higher good of the nation.

Kennedy had a view of politics similar to that of the Founding Fathers. He valued the traditions of civility of western civilization. He understood the need for politicians to follow their consciences rather than always follow the desire to retain one's office, please the party, or, even to follow the will of one's constituents. He knew that even the majority did not always choose the general good. In his book, *Profiles In Courage,* Kennedy described the courage of eight senators who followed their consciences in the face of public condemnation. These men acted according to principle, not self-interest. Kennedy went on to apply the same responsibility for courage to all citizens. In his closing paragraph he explained:

To be courageous, these stories make clear, requires no exceptional qualifications, no magic formula, no special combination of time, place and circumstance. It is an opportunity that sooner or later is presented to us all. Politics merely furnishes one arena that imposes special tests of courage. In whatever arena of life one may meet the challenge of courage, whatever may be the sacrifices he faces if he follows his conscience—the loss of his friends, his fortune, his contentment, even the esteem of his fellow men—each man must decide for himself the course he will follow. The stories of past courage can define that ingredient—they can teach, they can offer hope, they can provide inspiration. But they cannot supply courage itself. For this each man must look into his own soul.[11]

Kennedy's expectation that people should live by principle and have courage was the kind of expectation and message Americans wanted and needed to hear at the time he ran for president. He was calling us back to the public philosophy embedded in our collective memory by our idealistic ancestors. In his inaugural speech, when he asked Americans to give back to their country, he stirred up a dormant desire to replace self-interest with a higher calling. He had the ability to make people reach for goodness and to establish good character. Kennedy was one of those, as Lippmann said, "of light and leading" who made the public philosophy the "Mandate of Heaven." Of course, he had his imperfections. We will never know how far he would have taken the country towards restoring the traditions of civility. However, at that time in history many Americans perceived his message as one of high ideal, and they hungered to develop their higher nature and achieve a higher calling. He was a man for the times. He stood for the traditional principles of civility and service that could have returned our society to social and political soundness.

As a result of his death, thousands of young adults who had planned to enter public service turned away from government and politics. Many young citizens who were committed to public service out of good motives never served in our government. These idealistic individuals could have kept our country on the course towards a reevaluation of our values. They could have modified the materialism and consumerism that was on the rise. They could have restored some of the traditional values and traditions of civility that were fading. If they had succeeded in reforming our politics and restoring our traditions, we would not have seen the Hippie Movement burst out of the confusion and despair that followed soon after his death. He had provided new meaning to American lives; he had restored idealism and hope. The assassination of Kennedy made these young people give up their hopes for a better America. They disappeared into private life or into planting the seeds for the Hippie Movement. Since the reform did not occur, the modern liberal revolution was inevitable.

After Kennedy's assassination, their grief and shock sent Americans into a stupor. Hope was extinguished and direction was lost. The years that followed, with the deaths of King and Bobby Kennedy, reinforced Americans' feelings of powerlessness and despair. Although having power to stop the Vietnam War, most citizens no longer concentrated on their responsibility as citizens. During that time of shock and mourning, America was transformed. As mentioned above, after Kennedy was killed, the liberal left unwittingly moved away from the course set by him. It was a tragic and devastating choice that has set America on a course away from the public philosophy and has increasingly undermined our democratic institutions.

With Kennedy gone and Americans in mourning and shock, President Johnson began to define the liberal agenda differently in spirit and action from that of President Kennedy. Out of their feeling of impotence and concern for injustice, many liberals rebelled against everything they viewed as the "military-industrial complex" and "The Establishment." They erroneously connected the power elite with all things traditional. However, the traditions the liberals rejected had nothing to do with the power elite. In fact, their rejection of those traditions increased the acceptance by American citizens of the industrial philosophies. Liberals mistakenly advanced the destruction of the safeguards of our democracy by destroying the traditional principles that protected it from anarchy and despotism.

By the end of the 1960s, the Hippie Movement emerged out of the malaise of despair. The solution of the youth was not to fight the power elite, "The Establishment," politically. They decided to "drop out." Dropping out turned into more than a passive act. It became a rejection of all of the traditions that had held the fabric of society together. Hippies and the liberal left mistakenly associated the traditions of the civil society with the "military-industrial complex." The vision of President Kennedy was buried in the procession of self-love, self-absorption, and self-importance that followed the sixties rebellion. Every ten year span since the 1960s has been described as self-centered in some manner, whether because of the self-indulgent pop psychology of the 1970s, the greed of the 1980s, or the economic arrogance of the 1990s.

Liberals And The Power Elite In The Nineties

Not only did the liberals take society away from the public philosophy; they also adopted the same tools of deception in the media as were used by the power elite. In fact, in the nineties, Clinton, an admirer of Kennedy, became the model deceiver; he achieved near perfection in his ability to seduce his listeners into accepting any of his ideas or personal defenses. He outdid the Republican "dirty tricks" of the seventies and eighties. Since the end of the 1960s, the liberal Democrats have used the same Machiavellian philosophy as that of the economic conservatives— the end justifies the means.

The Uniting Of Factions At The National Level

Consequently, the American public is left with little representation. To varying degrees, the Republicans have been used through the years to support the policies of the power elite. Now, the Democratic Party is in the hands of the special interests that rule the liberal left. They have formed a coalition of minority special interests—feminists, gays, environmentalists, labor, teachers, and minorities—to create their own united factions. They continue to try to challenge the commercial power elite with their own power elite. If liberals win, the people still lose. No elite group acts for the general good. Elitists will only do what they believe is best for their people and their own causes. They will not promote the common good—what is good for the society as a whole. The other option of the liberal elite is to unite with the commercial elite and split up the power according to interests. Campaign contributions have opened the door to corporate influence in both parties. This seems to be the direction the Democrats in Congress and the Executive Branch are taking. Clinton has been very accommodating to corporations. Ron Brown, the Secretary of Commerce who died in a plane crash, was really more of a secretary of commercial and corporate interests in the global economy. If Clinton and the Democrats in Congress represent the plan of the liberal elite; then they have made peace with the corporate powers, and now both have their areas of power mapped out.

The Uniting Of Factions at the Local Level

There are signs of factions uniting locally as well. Many cities have been developing partnerships with special interest groups and businesses. They are trying to include all stakeholders as partners to run each city. Rather than hire city employees with city oversight to establish programs, non-profit foundations, with expertise in various areas, are given contracts to help the poor, provide housing, provide employment training, etc. There is a movement to unite various factions or interests in order to split up the pie of local contracts and influence. The representatives of the public, the mayors and city councils, are made to depend on bureaucrats and stakeholders to tell them what to do and how to do it. They are discouraged from leading and encouraged to be facilitators.

I recently attended a meeting of representatives from neighborhood advisory councils (community groups) from all areas in San Jose. We were asked about the problems in our neighborhoods. All of the representatives complained about being ignored by the elected representatives and bureaucrats at city hall. One person suggested they put pressure on the staff of elected officials to come to neighborhood meetings in order to keep the groups updated on future projects in their areas and receive feedback from association members. In that way the elected official could hear from those most active in the community. At the same time, the elected representatives could still receive feedback from other members of the community.

In contrast, another person at the meeting suggested the neighborhood groups pressure the city to develop a neighborhood advisory commission consisting of representatives from the neighborhood associations. The mayor and city council members would have to receive advice from this commission before making any decisions affecting a particular neighborhood. In this organizational form, the neighborhood groups would grow in power and influence while the majority of voters in that neighborhood would lose power. Neighborhood groups do not have large memberships and should not officially speak for the majority of citizens in their areas. If they were given increased power, they would join the insiders instead of remaining a watchdog on the outside. Citizens elect the mayor and city council; they do not elect the members of the neighborhood groups. It is the responsibility of elected officials to discover the will of their constituents as directly as possible.

The dependence upon commissions, organizations, and corporations who are the supposed experts can weaken the bond between a public official and the public. The recent trend to unite factions at all levels of government opposes the plan of our Founding Fathers to use factions to protect the people from any despot—the majority, an aristocracy, or a monarch. Without the public philosophy to keep the people alert and responsible, they have become dupes of the rich and the special interests. The various factions have learned how to reverse the process to favor themselves. I do not think the liberal left originally intended to go in this direction, but they sold out principle for power. They are part of the problem.

In Chapter Three we will explore the culture of the 1950s which was clinging to the last vestiges of the public philosophy. I will show the interconnection between the moral and civil elements of society. Then we will stop for a view of the conscience in order to understand how the loss of the public philosophy has created a moral dilemma equal to and connected to the political one. In Chapter Four we will more closely trace the history of the breakdown of our republican form of government and the principles of civility that ruled our society. We will see the complete flip of our culture from a responsible, knowledgeable citizenry to self-loving children controlled and continually distracted from the truth by a manipulating, parental government

Chapter 3.

The Culture That Used To Be

What is God-given is what we call human nature. To fulfil the law of our human nature is what we call the moral law. The cultivation of the moral law is what we call culture. (Confucius)[1]

Up until the 1960s, there was an identifiable American culture. Although there had been a weakening of self-rule by the power elite, the majority of Americans still held on to certain traditions of civility. It is true that self-interest and materialism had been mixed into the public philosophy of duty and sacrifice for the higher good, yet, the more traditional values were consciously supported and adhered to.

American civil and moral traditions had absorbed many cultures while retaining the defining elements of the original culture. The culture of each immigrant group was seen as a subculture. They contributed to the mainstream culture, but, at the same time, their subculture was ultimately "melted" into the larger one. The original American culture had a well-defined moral code. In fact, it was difficult to separate American political values from its moral ones since its Puritan founders combined both in their worldview. The forming of a free civil society with high moral principles was as important to the Puritans as forming a community in which the freedom of religion was protected. The civil and religious ideals were intermixed. Alexis de Toqueville, a Frenchman who interpreted the American experience for Europeans in the middle of the nineteenth century, pointed to the religious-political union as a defining quality of the American democratic experiment. He noted that "Puritanism was not merely a religious doctrine, but corresponded in many points with the most absolute democratic and republican theories." [2]

Toqueville further described the union of liberty and morality in America, "Liberty regards religion as its companion in all its battles and its triumphs,…It considers religion as the safeguard of morality, and morality as the best security of law and the surest pledge of the duration of freedom."[3] American culture was grounded and rooted in the pervasive intermingling of liberty and religion.

Added to this Puritan foundation, as mentioned in the first chapter, was the Enlightenment thinking that was popular during the time of the Founding Fathers. Enlightenment thinkers had ideas that were in conflict with some Puritan ideals; for example, they questioned the existence of original sin. However, both agreed human nature required "the molding and civilizing principles of education that had animated societies through history."[4] The Founding Fathers, although less religious than the original colonists, had a deep suspicion of human nature. They believed civilization created the structure, norms, and laws that brought the best out of human nature. Left to themselves, humans would follow the instincts of their lower nature. They set up the check and balance system in our republican form of government because they saw a need to protect all involved in governing from the corruption in their own nature.

Out of the wisdom and experience of our Puritan ancestors and Founding Fathers came the moral, social, and political ideals that formed the American culture. Up until the 1960s, the moral, political, and social elements of this culture were accepted by the majority of Americans. Within the culture, there were commonly agreed upon ideas: a) the common good was more important than individual good, b) manners and good etiquette were expected, c) honesty and integrity were highly esteemed, d) self-sacrifice for the good of others was encouraged, e) sex was wrong outside of marriage, f) abortion was murder and therefore outlawed (yet obtained illegally), g) homosexuality was considered perverted and wrong, h) divorce was criticized, i) single mothers were rare,

j) drug and alcohol abuse was frowned upon, and k) instincts and impulses needed to be restrained. Before the cultural revolution, people felt guilt and shame when they transgressed these commonly accepted moral standards. Overall, Judeo/Christian and Enlightenment principles provided the accepted norms that shaped our culture.

Personal Reflection on the Fifties

I was born in 1940. I was one of those blessed to go through high school in the 1950s. I graduated in 1958. My experience was probably more ideal than many Americans because I lived in a Southern California beach community. It was small, beautiful and safe. It could not have been more of a utopia for a young person.

My friends and I lived under and within the Judeo/Christian and Enlightenment moral code that pervaded our culture. We did not question these moral values. We knew we should be honest—not cheat, lie or steal—unselfish; respectful of all adults, calling them by their last names; display good manners; and never have sex before marriage. We often broke this moral code, but we never questioned its rightness. Our greatest "sins" were cheating in school (which we tried to correct by creating our own honor code), sneaking into the movie theater through the exit, cutting school now and then, letting the boys peek into the windows at our slumber parties, the boys getting drunk at parties, drag races in the countryside, and boys and girls necking up at the "top-of-the-world." All of these acts of disobedience were done with feelings of guilt and shame, depending on the degree of seriousness of our actions.

The girls knew they should not have sex before marriage. If they did have sex and became pregnant, most of them quickly married the boy who "got them pregnant," or they quietly left high school for a time or permanently. If a pregnant girl did not marry, the baby was usually secretly given up for adoption. It was rumored that a few pregnant girls had abortions. It was never spoken out loud to the general population and never confirmed with certainty. There was always silence when it came to abortions.

I remember one time the sophomore girls in my class had a slumber party, which I missed. On Monday morning, rumors were everywhere that the senior boys had crashed the party. Everyone started drinking and the sophomore girls were making out on the front lawn and in the house with these seniors. Our very stern math teacher heard the rumors and immediately called all of the sophomore girls who were at the party to a private meeting. She gave them a lecture on sexual morality and on the sexual behavior of senior boys. She warned them that their reputations were in jeopardy. These girls were never as vulnerable again to those boys.

Although the moral code was clear, probably twenty percent of the boys and girls in my class of one hundred students had sex during high school, especially the popular ones and the artistic group. I am not sure how accurate my perceptions were because those who were "loose" only talked about it within the group who were sexually active. Many of them were my friends, but because I was not one of those sexually active, they kept it a secret from me. I am only going by my impressions.

In evaluating that time, it could seem phony or hypocritical to have a moral code that many people broke. It may appear unfair that those who broke the rules were more disrespected and felt more shame than those who followed the rules. It was accepted that those who followed the rules were more virtuous than those who broke them. Is it unfair to judge behavior by a moral code? How does it work? Society has rules created by the beliefs of the culture. Every person has the free will to make a choice about following a moral code or not following it. Moral codes appeal to man's higher nature to do what is good. If the desire to be good is not a strong enough motivation, the fear of shame and guilt reinforces a person's desire to obey the moral code. When individuals choose to break the rules, they suffer the consequences of their actions; they experience shame, guilt and judgment. If they want to avoid those negative feelings, they can do so by obeying the rules and by working to change them if they feel they are unjust.

Of course, a moral code needs to be reasonable and fair, and there needs to be room for mercy and forgiveness. Everyone breaks the rules sometimes. Therefore, people need to remember their own human frailties and be ready to forgive and understand. Sadly, some people are not forgiving, and some people look for an opportunity to condemn others. Yet, in order to keep order and promote moral conduct, there have to be moral codes and norms with the use of guilt and shame by the conscience to promote obedience to them. Without moral codes or laws, the conscience, and shame and guilt; a society has to create more laws and stiffer punishments to keep order. Confucius, a sage in ancient China, understood the need to train the people in virtue. Without a virtuous citizenry, a government has to rule by force and laws. He expressed this idea when he said, "Guide the people with governmental measures and control or regulate them by the threat of punishment, and the people will try to keep out of jail, but will have no sense of honor or shame. Guide the people by virtue and control or regulate them by li (moral laws), and the people will have a sense of honor and respect."[5]

Some people question the moral superiority of the fifties. Minorities, especially African-Americans, suffered great injustices. They were unjustly killed. They were even kept from voting in the South. Yes, there were injustices then that do not exist now. However, the consciousness and consciences of Americans were just becoming educated to and aroused by those injustices. The application of moral standards is always evolving. Hopefully, every society becomes more virtuous as its citizens becomes more conscious of injustices and their consciences made more sensitive.

There are many examples of the evolution of the American conscience. The Abolitionists before the Civil War served the purpose of informing and educating the American conscience and consciousness as to the unjust and inhumane nature of slavery. They did not need to overthrow all morality in order to bring about the freeing of the slaves. They faced the struggle with courage, and they broke political laws that broke moral laws. They did not need to break moral laws and moral principles in order to achieve their goals. They forced political laws to conform to the moral ones. So too, the Civil Rights Movement accomplished similar goals through moral, not immoral means. In fact, King depended on the moral power of nonviolent, civil disobedience and upon the sensitivity of the consciences of Americans. In the end, that moral power succeeded in changing the American conscience and the Civil Rights Movement achieved its goals in the South.

In conclusion, the fact that the consciousness of Americans in the fifties was not completely converted to civil rights does not take away from the virtue that existed on other levels of consciousness. The consciousness and conscience of an individual or people can be very virtuous in some areas and ripe for change in others. One area of weakness does not negate all of the evolutionary, moral growth that has occurred in other areas. To deny the progress of American character in certain areas, because it is not yet perfect in all areas, is to undermine the self-respect and virtue that it took centuries for America to obtain. The fact that slaves were freed in America while slavery still exists to this day in some parts of the world and the fact that the Civil Rights Movement was successful reveals the righteous qualities existing in the American character. The excessive and purist criticisms directed by intellectuals and liberals upon the traditional parts of our American culture have robbed the United States of self-respect and virtue. Our "collective memory" has been distorted and disfigured, leaving Americans either cynical or defensive.

It cannot be said that the public philosophy we followed up until the fifties created a perfect world. Because it had already been diluted, it did not serve the nation as well as in the seventeenth, eighteenth, and early nineteenth centuries. Moreover, there were those who held these beliefs but did not live them. There were some that exercised judgement on others without compassion and mercy; and there were many who did not apply the Judeo/Christian and natural laws of love and justice equally to all. However, the American culture up until the late 1960s provided a moral and legal compass for ethical behavior and civil responsibility. There was a unified set of moral and civil principles and laws taught to American children. These moral principles and laws informed their consciences, thereby containing and restraining most of the excesses natural to human nature.

In the next section we will examine the conscience to see what it is and how the loss of the public philosophy has affected it. We will answer the questions: What happens when there is an impoverished moral code and public philosophy? What happens to the conscience when it is not fed traditions of civility? We have seen how the traditional principles have been eroded by the industrial and liberal philosophies. How has this changed or diminished the American conscience?

What Is The Conscience?

The conscience is the faculty dwelling within all humans that has the capacity to tell them what is right and wrong. The conscience can be understood by using the analogy of a guitar. The strings of the guitar make sounds when they are plucked, but the sounds are not naturally and always in tune. The strings have to be adjusted in order to tune the guitar. The strings are adjusted, loosened or tightened, to make them match certain universal, transcendent tones. The 'G' string on a guitar makes the sound or tone that duplicates the universal note of 'G,' and it can be duplicated by most instruments in some fashion. The important thing to notice is that the sound of the 'G' string must match a universal tone that is called 'G.' The 'G' string is tuned to the 'G' tone.

When we sing the song, "Happy Birthday," we try to start the song on the right note that everyone can sing. It is like we are picking a note out of the air that fits the beginning sound of the song. There is a note out there some place that is the right tone to start the song of "Happy

Birthday." (The reason most singing of "Happy Birthday" sounds so terrible is because not many people can find the right note.)

In like manner, the conscience can be seen as a guitar needing to be tuned. When a child is born he/she has a conscience, like a set of strings, but the conscience is not yet tuned. There are objective, transcendent principles of right and wrong, to which each conscience must be tuned for it to function properly in guiding a person's behavior. These universal, moral guidelines can be found in the teachings of many religions that look to God as their source. Others throughout the centuries have found moral standards by observing nature and social intercourse. American culture was built on a moral code formed from a combination of Judeo/Christian and Enlightenment (natural law) values.

Walter Lippmann expressed the complement between religion and reason in his work, *The Public Philosophy*: "The crucial point, however, is not where the naturalists and super-naturalists disagreed. It is that they did agree that there was a valid law which, whether it was the commandment of God or the reason of things, was transcendent. They did agree that it was not something decided upon by certain men and then proclaimed by them. It was not someone's fancy, someone's prejudice, someone's wish or rationalization, a psychological experience and no more. It is there objectively, not subjectively; it can be discovered. It has to be obeyed."[6]

Humans Are Moral Beings

The existence of the conscience points to the fact that humans are moral beings. No other created being has a conscience. Humans are the only beings who can know right from wrong and create ethical standards and laws based on transcendent principles or first principles. When these moral principles—honesty, love, responsibility, self-control, perseverance, forgiveness, respect—are introduced to the conscience, it becomes tuned to these first principles and can then cause a person to act in obedience to them. When a person does not act according to their moral knowledge, it is said that they are going against their conscience. Of course, in the late twentieth and early twenty-first centuries people do not so much go against their consciences as they do not have an informed conscience telling them right from wrong.

Although humans are moral beings, that does not mean they will automatically behave morally. Human nature, consisting of good and evil tendencies, needs moral principles and laws to bring moral order to that nature. Humans can only fulfill their moral being through appealing to and strengthening the good tendencies through moral training and rewards for good behavior and weakening the evil tendencies through using punishment, guilt, and shame. The conscience is the faculty which, when tuned to ethical standards, sends the appropriate messages of guilt and shame when a person acts unethically.

Confusion About Morals

Presently, there is a confusion about right and wrong. People are uncertain what food to give to the conscience. Many Americans have accepted the delusional idea that morals or ethics are subjective, relative and situational. They believe that an action is moral or immoral depending on the perspective of the one committing the act. Consequently, it can be possible that murder, lying, or committing adultery is value-neutral or morally right in one instance and immoral in another. There are no objective standards of right and wrong; moral standards have become subjective.

Many do not believe there are absolute, moral guidelines. I will address those arguments later. In order for the conscience to be educated as to what is morally right and wrong, there has to be transcendent moral standards. Practically, people can universally agree upon ethical values from a common sense viewpoint as well. People can agree that the moral principles of honesty, respect, trustworthiness, responsibility, and love, to name a few, are essential qualities of good character. However, without universal moral principles, the conscience cannot give clear, precise moral guidance. By teaching a child a set of moral laws and principles, the conscience becomes morally educated or tuned; thereby providing the knowledge of right and wrong and the shame and guilt needed, when necessary, to prevent immoral actions.

Confucius, the Chinese sage, had many thoughts about morality. He discerned by his years of observation, experience, and reading that there was a universal moral order. Here are few of his thoughts: "The life of the moral man is an exemplification of the universal moral order. The life of the vulgar person, on the other hand, is a contradiction of the universal moral order." "To find the central clue to our moral being which unites us to the universal order, that indeed is the highest human attainment. For a long time, people have seldom been capable of it."[7]

Moral Standards: Principles And Laws

Actually, a conscience is tuned by being taught a combination of the moral principles and laws that make up moral standards. In fact, moral principles determine moral laws. For example, the Ten Commandments are moral laws demanding moral conduct. When a person acts immorally (breaks one of the Ten Commandments)—lies, cheats, murders, commits adultery—these acts are determined immoral if they break the universal moral principles of honesty, respect, love, responsibility, faithfulness, and so on. Any act that disobeys a moral principle is morally wrong. If a person lies to protect someone from an unjust death, the action is moral because it obeys the moral principles of love, trustworthiness and loyalty. If a person lies to get ahead on a job, it is an immoral act because it disobeys the principles of love, trustworthiness and loyalty.

No action that disregards moral principles can be moral. Humans must have a moral code to define right and wrong behavior. In addition, there must be moral principles to guide the fulfillment of moral laws. These laws and principles are universal and transcendent just as are musical notes. When a moral code or moral principles are absent, there is no way to tune the conscience. When this human faculty fails to perform its moral function, citizens become lawless. We see this result in American society: incomprehensive kinds of violence have increased as moral food for the conscience has decreased.

Since humans have consciences and are moral beings, one has to conclude that whoever or whatever created that faculty created a specific food to nourish it. Moral relativism has failed and will always fail to nourish the conscience, resulting in violence and moral decay. For centuries, transcendent and traditional moral standards—moral principles and laws—have been the main nourishing food for the conscience, resulting in more contained, mannerly, orderly behavior than is seen in today's society. These ethical standards have not always been applied to all people equally or justly, but that was the result of human wickedness not inadequacies in the standard. If the most nourishing food for the conscience is a universal moral standard, then it stands to reason this standard exists objectively, just as musical tones have an objective existence. Human behavior should be directed and measured by this objective standard.

Comparison Of Moral Laws and Principles With Physical Laws

Transcendent moral laws and principles can be compared to physical laws. No one can break a physical law without suffering certain consequences. If a person jumps from a tall building, he will propel downward and not upward because of certain physical laws. So also, when we break moral principles, there are predetermined consequences. For example, if a person constantly lies, first, he will develop a very untrustworthy character. Secondly, others will begin to distrust him. Thirdly, his lying will lead to loss of relationships and possibly loss of freedom if he lies to authorities. These are predetermined consequences resulting from a person breaking a moral law. There is no guarantee on the timing of these consequences, but they are certain to happen.

Because a person is immoral or unethical, he will not with certainty suffer the loss of or be denied power, fame, or money as a consequence of immorality. Disobedience to universal moral laws does not assure those consequences. The losses of good character and of relationships are the only certain consequences of breaking moral laws.

Of course, if a person murders another, there are possible legal consequences. Still, if the person possesses a lot of money and sharp lawyers, he can still avoid rightful punishment. However, he cannot avoid the loss of good character and personal relationships. If he has a morally informed conscience, he will have feelings of guilt and shame. In other words, another consequence of breaking moral laws is loss of peace of mind. If a murderer or lawbreaker does not have a morally informed conscience, he will not feel guilt and shame, but will instead, blame others for his crime. He would have a sociopathic personality—a person lacking a morally educated conscience.

Disobeying Moral Principles and Laws

Another interesting aspect of transcendent moral principles and laws is that when one moral law is broken, all moral principles are broken. It is impossible to break any one of the moral laws of lying, cheating, stealing, murdering, or committing adultery without likewise breaking all moral principles, such as: honesty, trustworthiness, responsibility, respect, love, loyalty, faithfulness, self-control, etc. For example, when a person lies, he has not only been dishonest but he has also broken trust with those to whom he lied. He cannot lie and still respect the recipients of his lie; nor can he be responsible, loyal, or loving to the person to whom he lied. In the same manner, when a person commits adultery, steals, murders, or disobeys any moral law, he disobeys all moral principles. Breaking moral laws can be profoundly serious, and therefore, it is profoundly essential to educate and train children's consciences in order to prevent disruptions in their character and relationships as well as to prevent societal, moral breakdowns and the consequent uncivilized behavior.

Conclusion

In answer to the original questions about how the loss of the public philosophy has affected the consciences of American citizens, we have seen considerable evidence that their consciences have been dulled and hardened. The consciences of most Americans are out of tune. People who were born after 1960 and did not attend religious schools or have ethically conscientious parents, have not had any experience with the American culture based on the public philosophy. They have not been taught those traditions of civility handed down from our forefathers. Without these laws and principles people have lost sight of what is right and wrong and how to be good.

The Josephson Institute of Ethics surveyed 8,965 young people and adults during 1991 and 1992. They found by their data that young people of this generation are less ethical than the youth of previous generations. Some of the following statements reflect the affects of self-interest and self-love on this generation.

- *I believe that the standard of ethics has changed greatly in society. For me, personally, I am influenced more by the outcomes of my actions than if they are ethical or not.*

- *I do what I do for me, no one else. I couldn't care less about stepping on or hurting other people to get what I want to succeed. I don't want to change.*
- *I feel that in society us kids can pretty much live our lives in making some decisions on our own. I also feel like in school if we want to cut classes or cheat that is our doing, because its our education, nobody else's.*
- *Ethics and law are often confused. Ethics are nice, but the law truly decides what's right and wrong.*
- *I would like to be more tolerant to others but I look after myself first because I'm the only one that counts.*
- *My ethical system is something which is continually revised and in a state of flux...but it works for me and is irrelevant to what other people feel is ethical.*[8]

Chapter 4.

The Big Bang
Cultural Transformation

The Big Bang That
Revolutionized American Culture

In this chapter we will explore the combination of elements that transformed our culture and government. We will concentrate on the liberal ideas and influence, but we will also enlarge and deepen our knowledge of other philosophies that contributed to the confusion of the times.

We have seen how the industrial philosophies were used to impair the public philosophy. There is another philosophy that designed the ideas embraced and espoused by liberals. The Romantic philosophy of the eighteenth and nineteenth centuries provided the basis for the liberal or progressive movement of the twentieth century. It competed with Judeo/Christian and Enlightenment ideas for two centuries before becoming the dominant philosophy. It took from the 1960s to the end of the 1970s for Romantic ideas to move from a secondary to a primary position in the American consciousness. The Romantic, liberal philosophy, along with other amazingly diverse ideas and events collided during those years, rather like the big bang theory of creation. Various social, psychological, philosophical, circumstantial, communication and historical elements collided in the 1960s—creating a new, dominant worldview in American culture.

The cultural big bang produced a new mixture of traditional and Romantic/liberal ideas, with the Romantic/liberal ones taking precedence. This new cultural worldview replaced the traditional, moral value system that was inseparably intertwined with American secular institutions. This new culture provided new food or moral laws and principles for the conscience. These new values have been deficient in their power to restrain and correct the wicked tendencies in human nature. Consciences have grown ignorant of right and wrong and have hardened.

One of the major elements in the big bang, which formed this new American culture, was the Romantic philosophy. European Romanticism had it roots in eighteenth century Europe. Jean Jacques Rousseau (1712-1778) originated this philosophical attack on the western civilization. Other Romantic philosophers continued developing romantic ideas over the next century. This philosophy helped broaden the scope of government to include more of "the people." It was the philosophical spirit behind the French Revolution.

Although many in Europe still extol the virtues of the French Revolution, the freedom it obtained often expressed itself in anarchy. Many heads literally rolled in the first years of the revolution with repeated overthrows of one government after another, concluding with the rise of the charismatic dictator/emperor, Napoleon. The French never succeeded in forming a completely stable government until after World War II.

In contrast, the American Revolution provided a much more balanced, long-term form of democracy. Its ideas of republican democracy were drawn from the colonial, democratic heritage developed under the Puritan compacts and from the ideas of government formulated by Enlightenment philosophers. In spite of these major influences, the American Revolution was also inspired by some of the Romantic ideas. Many elements of Romantic philosophy have stirred the American imagination since the eighteenth century, continuing alongside and in the shadow of Judeo/Christian and Enlightenment thought. Transcendentalists and Mark Twain expressed Romantic ideas in their writings. "In the United States, our intellectual traditions include on the one side Cotton Mather, Jefferson, Madison, and Hamilton, with their suspicions of instinctive human nature, and on the other, Emerson, Thoreau, and Whitman, with their trust in the 'holiness of the heart's affections.' "[1]

The Romantic philosophy was built upon a completely different interpretation of human nature than America's traditional world-view. As mentioned above, the public philosophy was based on the view that human nature was a mixture of good and evil. The Romantic philosophical tradition was built on a belief in the goodness of human nature and everything natural. Because human nature and nature was seen as good, there were certain logical conclusions that followed from this premise: nature is superior to civilization; man's animal nature is more innocent than his rational nature; nature or the earth should be preserved and protected; instincts; feelings and impulses should not be restrained, but cultivated and set free. Consequently, structure and order hinder the expression of natural, creative impulses. Man, especially the common man, is made perfect in the state of nature. Each individual should be allowed to achieve personal fulfillment through freedom from civil laws, societal institutions, and norms.

Romantic philosophers extolled native cultures because modern civilization was the cause of violence and selfish behavior. To them, civilized man had fallen from innocence through his concentration on possessions, unnatural work, societal institutions, superficial manners and norms, and intellectual pursuits. "The idea that civilization has a corrupting rather than a benign, uplifting, virtue-enhancing effect on the young child is a distinct contribution of European Romanticism to American thought."[2]

Their initial premise that human nature is good leads to certain conclusions. For example, the laws and norms of society are unnecessary, causing superficiality and hypocrisy. Humans do not need absolute, moral guidelines; customs and traditions; religious, social and governmental institutions; and consequences for wrong behavior. In a just and fair society people, out of their innate goodness, will be good, fair and loving.

Children need to be raised in a free (permissive), healthy, creative environment, and they will define and reveal their educational needs (liberal educational theory), and behave properly. By restoring children to their natural setting and allowing them to be ruled by their instincts and emotions, they will obtain happiness and receive fulfillment. A further logical conclusion is that since instincts and natural impulses are good, the sexual instincts and impulses of the human body are good and natural as well. Sex should be freely expressed outside the institution of marriage and not repressed by moral beliefs that lead to unnatural inhibitions. These conclusions are obviously becoming the norm for American culture.

These Romantic ideas were clearly at the root of the choices Hippies made in the late 1960s to live together, and with nature, communally and harmoniously and to follow their natural, sexual instincts. The Hippie Movement, with its subsequent influence, was like a tsunami wave of Romantic ideas that had been building in force throughout the nineteenth and twentieth centuries. Suddenly, it bursts into every area of American life. What had been formulated and followed for centuries by some intellectual, artistic, celebrity, business, and political elites now surged into the public consciousness. People began to question the superiority of civilized life over primitive, natural existence without knowing the philosophical source for these questions.

When I was living in the Haight-Ashbury in San Francisco in the Summer of Love of 1967, this Romantic philosophy became a reality. I saw fifteen-year-old girls running around with bells on and barefoot, giving themselves to any man or boy that wanted them. It was free love. I saw the guilty looks on the faces of the men as they took advantage of these girls' drug-enhanced naivete. They conveniently adopted the free love philosophy, helping to unplug the consciences of these girls. One girl must have had sex with fifteen different men in the span of a couple hours. Each one came out of her room with an embarrassed smirk on his face. One young man said sheepishly that maybe she was sick and probably a nymphomaniac, but that didn't stop him. Sadly, this lifestyle and its cultural ideals were romanticized and promoted by the media in the following years, producing the immoral conduct, sexually and otherwise, that we presently see.

This philosophy was recognizable in Clinton's affair with Monica Lewinsky as well. Clinton was impulsive, lacking self-control. As a baby-boomer, he was raised with Romantic ideals about sexual freedom. He was a product of the Romantic ideas incorporated into liberal, modern thinking. He and Lewinsky followed what to them were natural, sexual instincts and impulses. Neither felt shame for their actions until they were caught. Then, they felt shame because of the emotion and shock of the media and reactions of moral citizens rather than shame for having done something wrong. Why else would Clinton feel self-righteous and justified in his attack on those who were judging and accusing him?

He had to have been conditioned by the general feeling in elite, liberal circles that sexual liberation is a positive accomplishment resulting from the moral questioning that happened at the end of the 1960s. During that time, drugs and free love became normal, acceptable behavior by many Americans. Vivid sexual scenes became common in movies and one-night stands were regularly presented as normal, amoral behavior. Today, very few parents have influence with their children, if it is their desire, to convince them they should abstain from sex until they are married. The societal attitude is that anyone who abstains from sex until marriage is inhibited and unnatural. This attitude is a complete reversal of the societal attitude present in the fifties and previously.

Hippie Movement Contributes To The Big Bang

Most Americans critical of our present culture point to the 1960s and the values of the Hippies as the beginning of our national, moral decline and cultural revolution. In actuality, the Hippie Movement expressed a worldview that had been germinating for more than two centuries. Who were the Hippies? Where did they come from? The Hippies were partly created by middle class access to a college education in the 1950s and 1960s. Large number of families, who had never had a college graduate, much less a high school graduate, suddenly had the opportunity to send their children to college. The huge middle class that came into existence after World War II inundated colleges with their children. For the first time in the history of the U.S., large numbers of its population were introduced into political, historical, philosophical and scientific thought earlier restricted to the aristocratic class.

These first generation college students entered a world previously unknown to their numbers. They entered this educational world with naivete and idealism. Since their parents did not possess the same knowledge they acquired, they lost respect for their parents. As they discovered the injustices and imperfections in the American system, they reacted with anger. Being less educated than their children, parents were not able to filter out any exaggerated and deceptive criticisms of American society. Yet, these new middle class college students did not have the life-experience to judge what they were being taught. College enhanced their ability to discover injustice in the society, but it did not give them the wisdom on how to best overcome these injustices. Instead, they headed out into unknown waters with a deep rage at injustice, which they turned against everything traditional.

These students directed their rage at the older generation, including their parents, and judged them to be hypocrites. They were being taught the American values of equality, freedom and justice, but they did not see their parents and government fulfilling these values. This perceived disconnection between values and actions caused the young to become disillusioned with authority. They became opponents of "The Establishment." In the process of rejecting the way of life and authority of the capitalist values, they rejected the traditions of civility that had defined the culture of the United States since its founding. In their minds being good and moral came to mean helping the disadvantaged, minorities, and mistreated rather than possessing traditional character qualities. Other moral principles, such as honesty, respect, sexual virtue, and responsibility; could be sacrificed to create a more just society. Their anger and rebellion set the stage for a small number of these students to join forces and begin the Hippie Movement.

Besides the contribution of college education to the Hippie Movement, there were other factors building up through the years. There was the Romantic philosophy mentioned above. Also, the increase of materialism and prosperity made American youth perceive the culture as shallow and empty. In reality, they were sensing the weakening of the public philosophy. They felt there had to be more to life than material success, but they did not know where to look for a more idealistic purpose. Many young people decided to drop out of society because they saw injustice towards minorities, distrusted the reasons for the Vietnam War, experienced the death of unselfish idealism in the death of John F. Kennedy, and developed a deep distrust for their parents and their government.

The Hippies went further than the Beatniks, who were the critics of America during the forties and fifties. They went beyond their criticism by dropping out of the consumer culture. "Dropping out" meant rejecting most traditional values. Hippies: refused to work; shared their homes, food, clothes, everything with anyone who needed it; lived communally; bathed less often to avoid the perceived Western obsession with cleanliness; appreciated nature; embraced the more passive, non-aggressive Eastern religions; free love (sex); and using hallucinogenic drugs to expand the mind. The Hippies "dropped out" of caring about the common good, the larger society, and, instead, started to concentrate on personal relationships and their own self-fulfillment. To them, civilized society and traditional values had suppressed individual decency. They sought to discover and liberate their natural goodness and innocence through drug experimentation and uniting with nature. They were definitely part of the Romantic element that altered American culture.

Moral norms were slowly and universally tossed aside after the Hippie revolution of the late 1960s. Although in proportion to the total youth population the number of participants was small, the Hippie ideals and lifestyle took deep root in the psyche and consciousness of all young people of that generation—what has come to be called the baby-boomer generation. Is it any wonder that the baby-boomers are the generation that has moved this nation into a culture dominated by Romantic ideas instead of the traditional Judeo/Christian and Enlightenment ideas?

Personal Reflections On The Hippie Movement

I first lived in San Francisco in the summer of 1964. I stayed with my sister while I was waiting to enter a Catholic convent in Santa Barbara. When I got off the train, a friend welcomed me by asking if I wanted to drop "acid" that night with her and her friends. A chemist from Los Angeles had brought up sugar cubes laced with LSD. LSD was still legal at the time, but I opted to be a guide. That was my introduction to the drug that was going to help transform the Haight-Ashbury by the summer of 1967.

My friend and her companions were a young group of Beatniks; they knew Allen Ginsberg and Jack Kerouak who were their older mentors. They were actually part of a group that would help make the transition from Beatniks to Hippies. I spent the summer being a guide on a number of acid (LSD) trips and hanging out with Beatniks who smoked "pot" or "weed" and criticized the materialistic way of life of Americans. Kennedy had just been killed the previous November, and his death had a definite effect on encouraging further feelings of disappointment and despair.

Since I had been a hopeful idealist when Kennedy became president, his death was a deep shock for me. I felt powerless to really help our country by entering government; therefore I decided to serve people by becoming a nun and a teacher. I remained in the convent for two years. The order I was in was going through upheavals over the modern changes imposed by Pope John XXIII. I left amidst this confusion and disorder, having no idea what to do with my life. My sister had sent me articles about the changes occurring in the Haight in San Francisco. These articles explained the decision Hippies were making to drop out of society because they felt powerless to change it. In my state of confusion and despair, I felt drawn to investigate the movement.

I rented an apartment a few blocks from the Haight-Ashbury district. I ventured over there, meeting a few people. At the time, the summer of 1966, it was a community based on sharing and giving. The ideas were communist, and its leaders believed in the goodness of human nature. If you had clothes, food, home, and drugs, you shared them with those who were lacking these things. In other words, those who had, shared with those who did not have. It was a complete reversal of the perceived materialism in America. The Diggers, a group of Hippies with altruistic motives, provided a free lunch every day in the park. They used old food given to them by the markets. The free medical clinic was established. Wonderful San Francisco bands played for free every weekend in the park. The goal was to drop out of this narrow, stifling, materialistic society and create a new society of love, peace, and sharing. "Acid" and "weed" were used to expand the mind outside of the narrow materialistic plane imposed by middle class American.

Sex was seen as a natural instinct that should be practiced freely and without inhibitions. Free love was a way to throw off what the Hippies perceived to be the twisted view of sex and the human body held by our Puritan ancestors. Once my husband and I visited a nearby commune in which people walked around naked smoking weed and hashish. Men and women there had multiple sexual partners. They had deadened their consciences and minds as part of an effort to remove shame from having sex freely. It was all very idealistic, animalistic and naïve.

I was in my mid-twenties and had done a lot of thinking about life when I became involved in the Hippie movement. I was not one of the fifteen and sixteen year olds who ran away from home. I did not agree with the emphasis on eastern religions or the sexual ideas—I was still a Christian—but I definitely felt an affinity to the Hippies' desire to drop out of society. I was happy to meet people who felt the same disappointments and the same disillusionment. I had begun to write poetry, so I entered into the scene with the role of a writer. The magic of those days lasted until the summer of 1967. As soon as that summer hit, things began to go downhill.

All of the excesses of the movement attracted what appeared to be every taker and user in the nation. Young people, pimps, drug dealers, the Mafia, fakes, and phonies all descended on the Haight-Ashbury. The selfish part of human nature came into prominence and free love became lust and lasciviousness. Drug use grew into addictions. Hippie drug dealers were killed by professionals. Women became sexual objects. New arrivals began stealing from homes provided for them for free, and violent people were attracted like leeches looking for fresh blood.

I was married by the summer of 1967 and living on Ashbury Street with my husband. During our first few months there, we were thrown into jail without any cause. A person "crashing" in our "pad" attacked my husband and chased him down the street trying to kill him. The minds of some of our good friends and relatives slipped away, never to return. The FBI raided all of the apartments in our apartment house, and the apartment house we lived in was shut down for code violations.

That was the final outcome of the Haight-Ashbury district and the Hippie experience. What had begun as an experiment in love, deteriorated to an obsession with drugs and sex. The lower nature won over the higher nature. The Hippie Movement was not the one glorified in the press. If there was ever an example of a society needing order and traditions of civility, it was the Hippie society. I watched it fall apart. I watched friends fall apart. It was not long after of the summer of 1967 that violence broke out, and the Bank of America boarded up and then moved out.

What truly amazes me is the number of ideals of the Hippie movement that have been adopted by the larger, American society. The Hippie principles of free love, the importance of self-fulfillment, universal drug use, the idealistic view of human nature, and communistic spirit of meeting everyone's needs have become part of American culture. The failure of this experiment should have shown liberals, who have become the promoters of these ideals, that these ideas and practices do not work. Instead, through glorification by the media, these ideals have increasingly determined governmental policies and our moral code. Consequently, we are increasingly experiencing the breakdown of order, just as the Hippies did. Our government, politicians, and liberal special interests have not changed their agenda on seeing the breakdown of social order. Instead, the solution to disorder and violence has become the increase of laws, jails, and police.

Other Philosophical Ideas In The Cultural Big Bang

Ideas have power. Philosophy has always had a great influence on governments and the masses. For example, Nazi and the Communist philosophies were used to build totalitarian regimes. The idea of salvation through faith and the "priesthood of the believer," expounded by Martin Luther caused the Protestant Reformation and planted the seeds for the popular democracies of the last three hundred years.

Because philosophy or ideas are so influential, it is of the highest importance that they are an accurate expression of reality. If the premise of the philosophy is inaccurate, it will lead to faulty, destructive conclusions. The Communist philosophy is an example of a philosophy with a faulty premise. Karl Marx based his philosophy on the belief that human nature was good. Therefore, humans could live for the good of each other, all work together for an unselfish goal, and rule themselves without governments or laws. You can see the Romantic influence in this philosophy.

In the end, Soviet Communism failed because the people failed to work industriously without the element of competition and the possibility for economic improvement. The failure of Soviet Communism proved that human nature is not altruistic and unselfish. People must be challenged, rewarded, restrained, and morally uplifted to get the best out of them. Their nature has the potential for goodness, but it has to be nurtured and balanced by other factors.

In the United States we have a belief that has the same faulty premise. The Romantic idea that human nature is good has taken hold in our country and is often expressed in our media. As a whole, Americans citizens do not consciously believe that human nature is good. If asked, most would say, "absolutely not." The inhuman crimes against Jews in World War II finally dashed that belief. Still, the social, educational, and political policies continuing to be followed are based upon that premise. Romantic ideas are like a chicken with its head cut off; although its premise is disproved, it continues to show great activity and power. That, in and of itself, is not the only problem. What we call liberalism, which has strong influence in the Democratic Party, is also deeply influenced by Romantic thinking. To call oneself a liberal during the time of the Founding Fathers had a very different meaning than today. Even the liberalism of John F. Kennedy would not match with the liberal ideas we have today. Those previous liberals had some reservations as to what extent human nature was good.

The accuracy of the perception of human nature is the key to a balanced political and national philosophy. One of the steps to undermining our traditional heritage has been through philosophy. Besides Romantic philosophy, there are other philosophies developed in the nineteenth and twentieth centuries that also hammered away at the Judeo-Christian and Enlightenment ideas. They attacked the idea of the existence of any God and any universal moral code. Darwinian, Nihilist,

Utilitarian, and Existentialist philosophers took God out of the equation for understanding life and the universe. For example, the theory of special relativity was used most effectively to undermine a belief in absolute, moral principles. It was a scientific theory formulated by Albert Einstein. He ascertained scientifically that the perception of space and time is relative to whether a person is observing an object moving through space and time or is traveling in an object moving through space and time. Time moves slower for the person in the object than it does for the one observing it; thus, space and time are relative. They depend on the location and perception of the person timing the speed of the object.

This scientific theory was unfortunately and unjustifiably absorbed into philosophy just as evolution had previously been thrown into the philosophic pot. And now philosophers illogically concluded: everything is relative, including ethics. They proposed that ethical or moral decisions were relative to the situation. There were no objective, moral absolutes or laws to guide and restrain behavior. In moral relativism, the subjective perception of right and wrong by a person in each situation determines whether or not an action is moral or immoral. During the 1960s and 1970s, moral relativism was promoted in all forms of the media and in many college classes. Therefore, situational ethics became the accepted approach to morality. The public easily embraced this idea because all humans would rather follow their instincts to embrace pleasure and avoid pain. If a philosopher can give people an excuse for doing what feels good, not too many people will resist being convinced.

The mixing of science and philosophy has been a common practice for philosophers since the beginning of philosophy. Aristotle used the empirical method to develop his philosophical ideas. Philosophy has proven to be very influential on the actions of people and governments throughout the centuries. Sadly, many philosophical conclusions are unfounded in reality and have misled citizens and politicians. The twentieth century political thinker, Sir Isaiah Berlin, revealed the tendency of intellectuals to experimentally combine fields of thought: "When some branch of human inquiry, say physics or biology, won notable successes by employing this or that new and fertile technique, an attempt was invariably made to apply analogous techniques to philosophical problems also, with results, fortunate or unfortunate, which are a permanent element in the history of human thought."3

In the final analysis of social and political movements, ideas, not people, are their motivating force. Therefore, it is essential that those ideas be true and based on reality. Nineteenth and twentieth century thought has not been very accurate. As mentioned above, the indiscriminate combining of science and philosophy undermined the idea of universal and absolute standards for ethical standards. Furthermore, certain psychological discoveries about the subconscious and shame were uncritically added to the philosophic pot. What came out was a very perturbing and bitter stew of unfounded and unproven speculation. Because it has the label of philosophy, most people, unschooled in philosophical thought, accepted those ideas unquestioningly.

Historically, when Americans accepted the relativistic attitude towards ethics, it undermined the ethical values that permeated and defined the American culture. Without ethical absolutes or universal ethical standards, individuals were left without a compass upon a sea of choices. Slowly, since the late 1960s and the 1970s, moral principles have been neglected and moral laws have been broken. Confusion reigns when people see their children act lawlessly. Yet, their children are only acting out what they see modeled by their parents, other authority figures, and pop heroes.

Psychology's Role In The Cultural and Moral Big Bang

Of course, anyone who wants to break moral norms wants to be able to do so without feeling shame or guilt. All of my friends in high school who were having sex felt shame and guilt. Some of them lost respect for themselves and others became defensive and angry. Shame is a tormentor. No one wants to feel it. However, without it, society is lawless and people become self-destructive and addictive. Societies have always used shame to protect themselves from the excesses of human nature, which undermines order. As mentioned earlier, if there is no conscience or shame, a state has to depend on laws and threats of punishment to keep order. Even then, when authority is not present, it is most likely that its shameless citizens will disobey the laws. Although shame has a positive role to play in individual lives and in societies, governments and people have abused and misused shame to assert domination or forced moral compliance.

Psychologists and educators, for the past forty years, have focused on the manipulative and negative uses of shame. Guilt and shame have been seen as culprits, causing mental illness and low self-esteem. Many educators and counselors have campaigned against teaching ethical values because they fear the presence of any guilt and shame, even when those emotions are necessary and deserved. "In the 1960s, however, American educators thought they had discovered an alternative to the hard work of character formation. But as it turned out, the approach they developed actually seems to undermine morality in children."[4]

Many schools have adopted value-neutral curriculum to replace the natural law or Judeo-Christian model. Educators have emphasized the need for self-esteem in place of the need for academic learning and character development. "The emphasis—as it was in therapy—was on feeling good about yourself and feeling comfortable with your choices. It was an approach which cast the teacher in the role of amateur psychologist and which turned the values education classroom into something resembling an encounter group."[5] It is true that misplaced guilt and shame can do great harm to the psyche. They cause people to believe they are to blame for things done to them, usually as a child, rather than blaming the perpetrator of the offense. Often, children who are molested or abused think something evil in them caused the perpetrator to violate them, or children can think their parents divorced because of something they did. These erroneous emotions can lead to years of depression and serious psychosis. These issues are outside of the role of the teacher in a classroom or the moral code of a society. It is up to psychiatrists, psychologists, and family counselors to help victims learn the truth and dispel the shame.

A whole society cannot throw out its moral standards for fear of enabling false guilt and shame. The caretakers in society can be sensitive to individuals who have been deceived and disabled by these misleading feelings. It is not the job of the whole society to conform all of its institutions to the mentally ill or emotionally unstable. Government has a responsibility to maintain order, and that can best be accomplished by maintaining a cultural moral code by which immoral behavior is punished through shame. It is better to have anti-social behavior controlled through the use of guilt and shame than to have to use punishment by incarceration and death. We have recently learned this lesson as we have had to build more prisons in order to incarcerate thousands of our youth.

The Popularization of Psychology: In the 1960s and 1970s pop psychology was in fashion. Its insights were simplified and fed to the masses. Psychological self-help books became as common as other do-it-yourself books. They showed people how to obtain happiness through self-fulfillment. People came to view the process of fixing their psyches as easy as fixing the sink or building a shed. Encounter type groups sprouted up all over the nation. The purpose of these groups was to make people more aware of their subconscious feelings. They got in touch with their inner child and sought healing.

The new awareness had some advantages. It became more common for couples having marital problems to seek counseling. The younger generation did not feel the shame that the older generations felt about going to a psychologist or counselor. They felt more comfortable with their feelings and learned to identify them and express them. Many marriages have been mended and families put back together with the use of psychology.

The detrimental side to this psychological flowering lay in the increase of self-love and self-absorption. Americans became self-analytical by concentrating on their past psychological suffering. Humans are very impressionable. They easily fall under the spell of ideas and self-centered interests. As individuals explored their subconscious minds and past sufferings, feelings of self-pity and resentment grew. They were then encouraged to yield to these emotions. In encounter groups they were told to "Let it all hang out." Participants surrendered to their emotional impulses, entering into expressions of extreme emotions. One catharsis led to another. Finally, by the end of the 1970s, emotions were spent and some objectivity returned.

What was left was a worldview that was internalized in the American consciousness. These amateur psychological insights made everyone oversensitive to all pain and created a belief that humans were psychologically weak and fragile. Since the 1970s, parents and schools have become overprotective of children. They have excessively concentrated on increasing self-esteem in children—even to the extent of neglecting to educate their minds. Adults became fearful to set boundaries and say no to children because it might hurt their feelings or scar their psyches. Discipline became lax, and children became disrespectful. Many teachers have complained in recent years of the disrespect of students in all schools, not just in the ghetto schools.

In their book, *The War Against Parents*, Sylvia Ann Hewlett and Cornel West express the damage pop psychology has done to the parental-child relationship. They claim "that in its more watered-down, popularized forms, psychology can be extremely damaging, particularly to the parental role and function. At the heart of the matter is the fact that in our increasingly therapeutic culture, external obligations, whether to parents, children, or community, are minimized, because they interfere with a person's capacity for self-love and self-realization."[6] These authors see pop psychology as encouraging an individual ethic that places self-fulfillment above public service, family or other important causes.

When children feel their welfare is more important than any other life goal, they will not be very good neighbors or citizens. They expect life and people to always treat them fairly. They expect to always be treated equally and justly. Adults have spent their time making them feel overly important and deserving of special treatment. When life or events do not go their way, they act out in an antisocial manner. When a society promotes unrealistic expectations in children for happiness, it is in danger of producing citizens filled with self-pity and envy. These are not the kind of citizens most desirable for any community. "Human societies...have persistently sought as far as possible to suppress envy. Why? Because in any group the envious man is inevitably a disturber of the peace, a potential saboteur, an instigator of mutiny and, fundamentally, he cannot be placated by others."[7]

Helmut Schoeck, in his book, *Envy, A Theory of Social Behaviour*, goes on to explain that egalitarian societies fail to prevent envy because there can never truly be an "absolutely egalitarian society..."[8] In fact, egalitarian societies increase the feelings of envy. Since its citizens expect to all be equal, they envy anyone who has any advantage or talent superior to their own. The tendency to give American children exaggerated feelings of importance and the right to never have to suffer injustice makes them more vulnerable to the emotions of envy and revenge. They easily resent anyone who surpasses them or ridicules them. In their exaggerated sense of having been wronged, because they feel so very important, they justify their acts of revenge.

For example, at the end of the 1980s and into the 1990s gang members were killing each other, not only over drug territory, but also because another gang member disrespected (dissed) them. They put respect for themselves above the value of a human life. In addition, the tragedy at Columbine High School was caused because the killers envied athletes and resented athletes for disrespecting them. They wanted revenge. Surprisingly, in schools across the nation, counselors have been trying to sensitize children to the hurt feelings of outcasts instead of letting all children know that no one is so important and deserving of respect that they have a right to take a life. The emphasis on sensitivity training instead of character building will only magnify the degree of egocentricity and self-importance that has been bred in our children.

Psychology not only tells us that rejection damages a child's psyche, it also tells us that children need boundaries in order to feel loved. Children will keep testing authority until someone stops them. If no one stops their rebellious, impulsive behavior over too long a time, they will cross a line and it will be too late. They will have tasted power beyond the scope of their age and authority. With that taste, they become addicted to their perceived power and cannot stop themselves. Usually, only an overdose of drugs, a jail sentence or death can stop them. Hopefully, some punishment will turn them around before they do extreme damage to others and/or get themselves killed.

Personal Reflections On Psychology

I had never had much of an interest in psychology before or during college. I took only three courses of psychology. In the 1970s when I joined a Christian group during the Jesus Movement, I became more interested in it. The Christian group my husband and I joined sought spiritual growth through counseling and, what was called, discipleship. First, I combined spiritual and psychological principles to seek answers to my own motives and choices in life. This led to a degree of self-analysis and probing of my subconscious. Many of the answers I found helped me to become psychologically and spiritually healthier. I was able to obtain some healing of past memories and overcome feelings of false guilt and shame.

After growing spiritually, I was put in the position of a counselor for a number of women. During this time, and for the next twenty years as a counselor, I have encountered all of the attitudes I mentioned above. The most difficult obstacles to emotional health and spiritual growth were self-absorption, envy, and self-pity. It was extremely difficult to take people's focus off of their own personal suffering and direct their attention to the suffering of Christ for their sins. Much of the counseling was like a journey through a maze that continually returned to resentment towards God for having allowed them to suffer. They made spiritual progress, but often it was hampered. They seemed to have no sense of the years of American tradition and the centuries of Christian tradition that viewed suffering as a means for the development of good character.

Americans had always idealized good character as the highest human goal. Good character was proclaimed to be more important than status or material success. Americans knew there was no guarantee of long life or fair treatment. Sometimes during the colonial and pioneer days, more children died than lived. Many women died in childbirth. They were determined that nothing would stop them from settling this land, not for themselves, but for their posterity. Of course, I am describing an ideal that was rarely reached, but it was how Americans saw themselves. I found little of this traditional way of thinking in those I counseled. Weaknesses and sinful human nature are some of the reasons for their self-centeredness, but the humanism, which made man the center of existence, created some immovable spiritual and psychological patterns.

In the next section we will see how the message of President Kennedy was directed at correcting the weakness creeping into the American character. He felt strongly that Americans were becoming self-centered and soft. To our detriment, we have not seen the fulfillment of his vision since his death.

The Importance Of The Death Of Kennedy

When John F. Kennedy won the election for President in 1960, his message was exactly what the nation needed. As has been so often quoted, he said, "Ask not what your country can do for you. Ask what you can do for your country." He sensed it was time to call our citizens into service and sacrifice for each other, our country, and the world. He saw a weakness in the American character, which had developed from the end of World War II and continued on through the fifties. Americans had become self-indulgent and soft because of their extraordinary abundance and prosperity. He reminded Americans it was time to give back to the country in repayment for all it had given them; he asked them to sacrifice their own interests for the public interest. He appealed to their higher nature, and they longed to fulfil his dream and their own potential to be good. Unconsciously, they hungered to restore the traditions of civility and national purpose that were waning.

When Kennedy was killed, the dream of citizens entering public service died with him. The idea of contributing to the common good instead of to one's own immediate desires faded further from the American consciousness. The death of Kennedy was the most dramatic turning point in American history in the twentieth century. Without the accomplishment of this timely improvement of the American character, the nation moved towards further individualism and divisiveness. Many of the intellectuals and leaders connected to Kennedy's vision lost hope and direction, and they failed to lead the country back to the public philosophy.

Arthur Schlessinger, Jr., who was in the Kennedy administration, explained the loss to the nation by Kennedy's death in a theory about cycles of public service. In his book, *The Cycles of American History*, he describes two aspects of a repetitive cycle in American history. There is an interchange between "private interest" and "public purpose." Kennedy called a generation to public service. He inspired them to be unselfish. Kennedy's death interrupted the public purpose part of the cycle, and the generation destined to participate in government dropped out. Schlessinger predicts the generation of despair will break into the present selfish cycle and bring back the balance that was lost by the death of Kennedy. I hope he is right. Unselfish service, reinvigorated by those initially inspired by Kennedy's message, would be a healing balm for our nation.

After Kennedy's death, the nation went into a state of grief, confusion, and shock. President Johnson, who was politically further left than Kennedy, took the country in the opposite direction. He believed in expanding government's role to act for the people rather than the people serving each other and their government. He increased Entitlements and the attitude of entitlement. The liberal approach of Johnson stunted the cycle of public service and responsibility that had been introduced by JFK. Without the correction of our national character and conscience, special interests moved into the vacuum and demanded their rights. Many patriots who planned to enter public service turned to other occupations. I personally know people in my generation who were inspired by Kennedy to go into public service but no longer chose to serve in government. In fact, those people are still unable to speak about President Kennedy without tears coming to their eyes—myself included. We did not end up giving back to our nation the way we had intended.

Instead of people serving their country, under the Johnson administration, the government increasingly became a tool of special interests. Political power began to shift out of the hands of the many, the majority, into the hands of the few, the united minorities. Johnson used the government to create laws and programs to change the status and conditions of minorities. Not that all of those laws were wrong. Justice was long overdue. What became harmful was the practice of the government becoming the arm of special interests. Rather than our citizens becoming personally involved in changing society and becoming more unselfish, they became more self-centered and demanding. Every group who experienced injustice organized and began to use the media to promote its interests and lobby the government for laws and programs to enhance their causes. Every group focused on its own needs and not the needs of others or the needs of the country as a whole, the common good.

Personal Reflections On
The Death Of Kennedy

I was a sophomore in college when the then Senator Kennedy ran for president. I was majoring in political science and intended to go into law and later into politics. I was very idealistic in my desire to fight injustice and contribute to my nation. I had read Kennedy's book, *Profiles In Courage*. In it, he described Americans in government who had sacrificed reputation and popularity for the sake of doing what was right for the country. I respected Kennedy for the values he extolled in his book, and I decided to campaign for him. I was greatly encouraged and filled with hope when he won. I felt he would lead the nation on the right path.

When he gave his inaugural speech, I knew I had made the right choice. He made me feel good about wanting to serve our disadvantaged citizens and to serve the country. I felt there was hope for the nation to right the wrongs that were in our society. Now I know why I felt as I did. It took me thirty-nine years to discover the reason I was stirred by his message. I finally realized I was hungering to do what was right and to serve my country. Somehow I sensed there was something missing in our selfish, materialistic society. I felt its shallowness and longed for the values of the public philosophy.

I believe that President Kennedy had the right ideas for our nation at that time, and he had the right way to accomplish them. He had sized up the state of our character and found us lacking. Yet he had a strong belief in the ability of the American character to rise to a higher level of goodness. Many Americans, especially around my age, identified with his goals and vision. That is why, after more than thirty years, Americans still feel dissatisfied and unsettled about the conclusion of the Kennedy era. The dreams of Camelot still reside in our collective memories and subconscious. We went through that time of ecstatic hope and devastating despair together. There has never been closure to the Kennedy tragedy because the Kennedy legacy has not been fulfilled. When John F. Kennedy, Jr. died recently, it rekindled the memory and hopes of those who yearned for Camelot. Many people realized they had hidden hopes that the son would fulfill his father's legacy.

We are wrong to have looked to a living relative of Kennedy to carry out the dream. It is not up to living relatives unfamiliar with the original vision. It is up to those who were initially galvanized by the Kennedy message. In them there is a seed of the original legacy that needs to be brought to fruition. They are the children to whom the mantle has been passed. It is their calling to motivate the younger, post baby boomer generations.

There are many talented people in this nation who have been holding back or been lost in confusion. The Kennedy message is simple: give instead of take; love instead of hate, unite instead of divide, courage instead of cowardice. His legacy is the restoration of the main principles of the public philosophy. In Camelot it was "All for one and one for all." Who could forget the noble dream to which we were willing to dedicate our lives? It is not too late to turn back the tide of self-indulgence and self-love. We can still serve our country by appealing to the higher nature in Americans, lead them back to the fork in the road, and help them take the right path—the path to a common national purpose and a willingness to serve the common good.

Chapter 5.

Special Interests Undermine American Culture

Noble Movements Used Noble Means

What is wrong with the self-interest activities of special interest groups? Don't they have a right to use any means necessary to achieve a just end? Traditionally, the movements that have had the greatest success and made the greatest contribution to America are those movements that have had noble goals and used noble means to achieve them. The reformers in these movements have put the welfare of the whole nation as their first motive. The Revolutionary War, the Abolitionist Movement, and the Civil Rights Movement placed the good of the whole nation and the world above self-interest.

The reformers in these movements believed in the God-ordained destiny of America. America was an instrument of God for the good of all mankind as well as a home for all who hungered for freedom. Benjamin Franklin expressed his vision for America during the Revolutionary War, "Tis a common observation, that our cause is the cause of all mankind, and that we are fighting for their liberty in defending our own. Tis a glorious task assigned us by Providence; which has, I trust, given us spirit and virtue equal to it, and will at last crown it with success.[1]

King envisioned a most righteous goal for the Civil Rights Movement. He saw the American Negro as the "conscience of America—we are its troubled soul—we will continue to insist that right be done because both

God's will and the heritage of our nation speak through our echoing demands...We are simply seeking to bring into full realization the American dream—as yet unfulfilled."[2] He and many reformers in our nation held up a higher vision and higher goals to enhance the human spirit. These reformers inspired the good, unselfish and heroic qualities of human nature to obtain a righteous objective. Both their means and their end were moral.

The Civil Rights movement in the 1950s and 1960s improved the quality and character of American Society. It took another step towards providing equality for all races, genders, and ethnic groups. It began by King taking the Judeo/Christian principle of unconditional love— 'agape'—and holding it up as a mirror to Southern whites. He showed the hypocrisy of Americans claiming to have a country founded on Christian principles while denying equal rights to African-Americans. He expressed the moral power of 'agape' through non-violent, civil disobedience. Through the use of moral power, shame and guilt rose up in American consciences, and consequently, the South was integrated in a short period of time.

It was a totally positive period in American history. Not positive as far as the unjust resistance of the southern states, but positive in the selfless, righteous actions of the non-violent demonstrators. They were an example of what is best about the United States. They called out the moral best in the majority of Americans who supported their marches and sit-ins.

The Black Power Movement

The Black Power Movement interrupted the Civil Rights Movement, and what followed did not call out the best in human nature. As young black citizens became more conscious of the injustices imposed upon their race, even since the Emancipation Proclamation, many of their hearts were filled with bitterness, envy, outrage, and self-pity. This new awareness, with its accompanying rage, caused them to use violence to bring about change. An angry and demanding spirit replaced the moral power of love and non-violence. Psychology had recently focused on the human need for self-esteem. It showed how unjust and cruel treatment could make people weak and destroy their capacity to succeed. The more aware African Americans became of this human need for self-esteem, the more outraged they became with past unjust treatment.

Their mood change was completely understandable, wrong, but understandable. The increase of psychological knowledge opened the door for an increase in envy and self-pity. With envy and self-pity ruling in the hearts of many young black men and women, there was little room for forgiveness. Rage and revenge dominated this segment of the black population. In fact, anger grew in all minorities towards the majority as more knowledge of the need for self-esteem became common knowledge and the liberal philosophy of self-love became more prevalent.

Personal Reflections On Racial Rage

I met my former husband in 1966. He is African-American, I am Caucasian. We married in 1967 to the chagrin of both sides of the family. Being from two different races did not cause many personal conflicts in our marriage because we saw ourselves as members of the human race, not one particular race. We always saw our relationship as normal. Because we never considered our marriage unusual, most people responded to us in the same way. Consequently, our nuclear family did not experience very much observable prejudice.

The prejudice we experienced was probably evenly expressed between both blacks and whites. Most of the prejudice towards me, which came from whites, was mainly from the white, male coaches of my sons. They resented seeing a white woman with a black man. I experienced the same prejudice from black women. There were a number of times African-American women told me off for marrying "one of their men." They felt they had ownership of black men, and I had trespassed onto their property. All prejudice is founded in envy.

I have never been able to understand racial, gender, and ethnic prejudice. We are all children of the same God. He created us one human race with one human nature. Humans, because of their imperfect human nature, make distinctions that don't exist. If human nature were good, it would not make any distinctions. It would view people as God does: each one specially made for a preordained and important purpose for the good of all. We would see that we all need each other to accomplish our God-given purposes. Since the 1960s, Americans have experienced an increase in the separation of some groups in society against others. Some factions have united—people of color, women, gays, and environmentalists—but the distance between them and Conservatives has grown. Each side exaggerates the conspiratorial nature of the other. If we do not work together as one, for a common purpose, we will split this nation into unyielding, divided parts.

The Feminist Movement

There are two kinds of movements against injustice: One comes from the public philosophy, and has unselfish goals, which appeal to people's higher nature; and the other has selfish goals, which appeal to people's lower nature. The second one allows envy and self-pity to draw its participants into self-centeredness, bitterness, and rage. As mentioned above, The Black Power Movement and those who continue to advocate for blacks from selfish motives, are parts of the second kind of movement. Likewise, since the 1960s, envy and self-pity have increasingly motivated the Feminist Movement. Rather than appealing to the higher nature of women, movement leaders appealed to women's lower nature. The leaders of the movement let their envy of men bring out the worst in them. They told women they had a right to have everything that men have. They tarnished their goals for equality and justice by lowering their standards to match the standards of men. Although not morally superior by nature, for centuries, women had previously been the preservers of spiritual and moral standards.

Feminists' desire for equality expressed itself in the most corrupt manner in the area of sex. They envied men's opportunity to have multiple sexual experiences with a limited amount of shame and guilt. Society had always minimized men's sexual escapades while condemning and judging women's harshly, which is unfair. Women-libbers wanted to pursue their sexual feelings and lust the same as men, without harsh, moral judgements. In other words, they wanted the opportunity to develop and model the same poor, weak character as men in the area of sexuality. They wanted equality with men in pursuing their lower, instinctual nature. Sometimes envy blinds people to seeing that their desires are self-destructive; many women experienced this self-destruction during their participation in the loose sex of the 1970s.

Since the 1960s, in order to be more like men, women have relinquished their distinguished role as the nurturer and protector of the young. Since men could have sex and not experience any physical consequence, beyond sexually transmitted diseases, women campaigned to remove their physical consequence—having babies. Now, a woman can choose to have sex, and if she becomes pregnant, she can refuse to take responsibility for her choice to have sex by having an abortion. She now has the same option as a man to avoid accountability for the consequences of her sexual choices. It used to be that men could refuse to take responsibility when they "got a woman pregnant." Now women can avoid the same responsibility. Women have relinquished their role as preserver and protector of the young. Sadly, many women lost sight of their motherly role in society. They could have achieved some of the more righteous goals of the movement without selling out the essential contributions women make to maintain a civil society.

Women have achieved more equality with men, and I have experienced some of its benefits, but at what cost? Life is filled with injustice. The elimination of injustice should be a common goal of humanity but not at the expense of self-respect and good character. There are always noble ways to achieve noble goals; noble means usually demand more time and more sacrifice from the participants. Evil can only be overcome with good, and goodness is always tested in the fire of suffering. Moral power is the only weapon that can defeat wickedness and injustice without leaving a bitter aftertaste.

Personal Reflections On The Feminist Movement

I was in high school from 1954-1958. During this period the transition from the traditional view of women to the modern view was taking place. College was a natural, next step for most of my friends and me. For many of our families, we would be the first to go to college. I felt encouraged by my parents and teachers, but it was difficult to think beyond traditional gender roles. When I told my Mom I wanted to be a lawyer and go into politics, her response was: "Teaching would be a really good occupation for you." She meant teaching would be an acceptable occupation for a woman. She never could envision me outside of a traditional job.

One woman teacher believed in me. As the result of her encouragement, I ran for student body president and won. I was the second girl since its founding to be president of my high school. The other girl had been president about twenty years earlier, so this was a rare and special time for me and for my school. Feeling threatened, the boys in my class had campaigned for a male candidate. Since I had known most of them since kindergarten, the competition didn't get out of hand. After I won, the boys adjusted. Still, it was not the same as it would be today. Today, a girl being an ASB president is common in middle school and high school. At that time, it was very rare.

The teacher who encouraged me to run for school president also told me to follow my dreams. She said she believed I could achieve anything I set my mind to. Interestingly, as I went through college with good grades and leadership accomplishments, no one, male or female professors or counselors, gave me direction or encouragement equal to that high school teacher. If it had been in the eighties or nineties, I believe I would have received much more support and direction from college professors.

My daughter is now in law school. I have greatly encouraged her from the moment she showed an interest. She is married and has two children. Her husband completely supports her decision, and he is postponing further education for himself while she attends law school. He watches the children while she goes to school at night. This scenario would have been very rare in the 1950s or 1960s. There has been an increased sense of equality between men and women in the generations born after the 1970s.

Comparing my daughter's life with mine reveals a cultural change for women. My daughter's life shows the positive changes that have occurred since the 1960s, and partly, because of the Feminist Movement. There have been many improvements in the opportunities, expectations, and education for women. Women have become more assertive and less passive in accepting sexual harassment and other injustices. On a personal note, some books that explored women as victims have helped me throw off the shame and fear of rejection I would feel if I excelled over men. When I was young, I would hold back some of my abilities in order to please a man in whom I was interested. Therefore, I feel grateful to feminists for some of the women's causes they pushed forward.

On the other hand, their more righteous goals could have been pursued and achieved with fair and honest methods instead of abandoning principle for social gain. The women's movement has been inconsistent and double-minded. They have condemned behavior by some men that degraded women while ignoring the same behavior in men who supported their agenda. Their example of duplicity is a wrong model to hold up for the girls and young women in this country. The fact that the majority of women supported Clinton during the Lewinsky scandal reveals their ongoing lack of self-respect. It reveals their continued emotional vulnerability to charismatic men.

If feminists would like to be truly helpful to women, they would model behavior for new generations of women on how to become independent and self-confident without reference to men, negatively or positively. Most women continue to depend on men to define their value. Women still believe that their sexual desirability is the most important aspect of their worth. Feminists could help break down these lies and assist women in seeing themselves as complete and valuable in their own being. Only then, will women be more resistant to the charm and deception of a charismatic, male leader.

Besides feminists failing to increase the value of women in male-female relationships, they have also undermined the value of children and mothering. Raising children makes more of a demand on skill, intelligence, and character than any other activity in life. In recent years, girls have been raised to devalue the importance of motherhood. Many women are no longer satisfied to stay home and raise their children. Often, women will have a baby and soon after leave their child with a day-care provider and go back to work. When a mother works from choice and not necessity, she is neglecting her child.

I experienced the same neglect in my childhood and know how destructive and painful it can be. The worst years of my childhood were when our family moved to a new town, and my parents bought a combination restaurant and bakery. They spent long hours in the business, leaving my sister and I alone. I was in third grade. For the first three months, I cried every day at school. Previously, I had been well adjusted, fun loving, and a leader. In the three years my parents had the business my personality changed. I went from being outgoing and confident to becoming serious and rigid. I felt unsafe and unloved.

Before my parents bought the bakery, I had not suffered any traumas. During this time of neglect, I was threatened by a boy who wanted me as a girl friend, nearly molested by a convicted child-molester, and in daily conflicts with my older sister. Without our parents present to regulate our conflicts, my older sister used her size and strength to intimidate me, and I resisted her passive-aggressively. The safety, peace, and predictability of our lives vanished. As the lonely years passed, I started to believe (unconsciously) that my parents did not love me. Later, I was able to reverse the lie of their rejection in my mind, but that belief interfered with my establishing a stable life in early adulthood.

Besides my own personal experience with neglect, I spent twenty years counseling troubled people. So many people in our society are mentally and emotionally damaged, and the ones who are the most difficult to help are those who were neglected and/or spoiled. Psychological research has shown that children who are neglected have a less developed conscience. They have less ability to empathize with others and to know right from wrong. It is difficult for them to imagine anyone's pain but their own.

If you add spoiling onto neglect, you can create self-absorbed, unfeeling adults. This is a formula for creating sociopaths. Because many working parents feel guilty and ashamed for neglecting their children, they overcompensate for the neglect by giving their children things instead of love and attention. The people who I found the hardest to help through counseling were those whose parents gave their children money and things instead of time. These children have to find something to fill the holes left by neglect. Most often these empty places are filled with addictions, depression, pornography, solitary introversion, torturing animals, or a fascination with the perverse. When I counseled them, their self-pity, envy, and feelings of entitlement were so great, they wanted someone to make them well. They would not take responsibility for working to get well.

To avoid neglecting their children, my daughter and son-in-law had to make a decision about their lifestyle when they had their first child. I am very proud of their choice. They decided to live in an apartment and cut down on expenses, so my daughter could stay home full time with the children. She has always been independent and career-oriented, but once the children came, she knew her responsibility was first to her children. She has been dedicated to them, and they will never doubt they have been loved. Also, since she is home full time, she is able to train their consciences by spelling out what is right and wrong many times a day. When both parents or single parents work, these parents have only about two or three hours a day to form the character of their children.

My daughter says that the family situation for most of the children she sees at the parks is unhealthy. She lives in a highly professional community in Silicon Valley. Most of the parents both work and leave their children in day-care or with nannies who cannot speak English very well. Their children are often ignored by their nannies and left on their own. Many of the children do not know how to share and have not been taught basic manners. When the parents are with them on the weekends, they act like they are strangers trying to play at being mom and dad.

The effects of the Feminist Movement, both on born and unborn children, are devastating. As the result of feminist influence, the majority of American women have taken freedom and self-fulfillment to unhealthy limits. Much of the violence we are seeing among children is the result of the breakdown of the family, most often by parental neglect. Children are weak and innocent; parents have a responsibility to love and protect them. They cannot turn their children over to the "village." It is rare to find people in the "village" or through the government who will love and care for children with the same personal dedication and sensitivity as parents.

Families have to raise children. America needs healthy families. Women are able to develop self-esteem, self-confidence, and a sense of equality while being mothers. They can have a career and raise children successfully by planning their future. They can fit in everything if they are willing to take more time in their lives to fulfill their goals (have a career later or have children later). Raising good, healthy, and happy children is one of the most satisfying and character-building activities anyone can ever perform. In addition, successful child rearing is a service to the community and to a democratic society.

The Gay Movement

The lesbians and gays in American society jumped into the stream of minority rights by the 1970s. This group has benefited from this country's move towards sexual liberation. They began to use the techniques of other minorities, using the media and politically correct mind conditioning. They have recently claimed to be a genetically created minority, using a scientific study that has never been able to be duplicated. If it could be proven that the great majority of gays and lesbians are genetically predetermined, then it would be society's obligation to ensure them all of the rights of all citizens and other minorities. If they have no choice but to be gay, then, logically, it follows they should also be able to marry someone of the same sex. They should not be denied the right to have a family.

If a group of people is a minority by birth, they should not be denied the rights of other citizens. On the other hand, if gays are a minority by choice, then they have no other rights or privileges than people who choose to wear a nose ring, dye their hair green, or wear black lipstick. Any subculture, which is a subculture by choice, does not have the rights of a legal minority, such as, racial and ethnic minorities and the disabled. These other groups are not a subculture by choice.

Those who choose to create and participate in a subculture should expect to receive social criticisms. They should not be mistreated or harmed. But they should not expect to have many job choices if they display sub-cultural dress or styles. If they live outside of the moral or social code of the mainstream culture, they should not demand that their employers give them benefits that are intended for married couples. Expecting employers to provide benefits for a gay partner or any unmarried partner undermines the sacred and institutional nature of the marriage contract or covenant. Minorities created by choice have chosen to live a certain way, and they have a right to live that way, but they cannot expect special treatment or institutional benefits because of their decision. They should not carelessly dismiss the idea of the institution of marriage that has been present for centuries.

One of my sons was a member of a subculture of skateboarders. He and his friends used to dye their hair a variety of bright colors. He complained that people would stare at him. I told him if he didn't want people to stare at him, he should dye his hair back to its original or some normal color. I explained that he was behaving differently than the mainstream culture, so he stood out. If he didn't want to stand out, he needed to look like others in order to blend into the mainstream culture. I further explained that it was time for him to get a job, and I feared his bright green hair might prevent him from getting a job. I explained that to be hired on most jobs, you had to relinquish some of your sub-cultural ways. He could always hang out with friends after work and continue to participate in his subculture, but when on a job, he would have to take out the nose ring, hide the tattoo, and return his hair to its normal color.

Gay men and lesbians are in the same category as those who choose to identify with any subculture. They should not be mistreated, but if they make a display of their sexual preference, people will notice. It should not be their goal to change the mainstream culture to conform to their subculture. In fact, it is extremely arrogant for them to think that they have a right to demand that the mainstream culture should change just for them. Paula Martinac recently wrote an article in the San Jose Mercury News, which showed the arrogance of some gays. She complained because Americans "believe that lesbians and gay men deserve basic civil rights—say, fairness in housing and employment—but they draw the line at marriage."[3] She admitted that Americans' resistance to gay marriage stems from their moral beliefs. Furthermore, she understood that gay marriage threatened a "social and economic setup" as well as "the fabric of society" in this country. Even with this evidence that the mainstream culture still clung to traditional values in the area of marriage, she concluded that the mainstream culture should adapt to the gay culture.

In the article, Martinac described the path gays and lesbians should follow to change the mainstream culture. It is a very clear description of the tools and practices used by many minority groups to manipulate and confuse the minds of Americans. Their goal is to change the American culture to fit the agenda of their subculture.

Martinac wrote, "Instead of fighting for—and losing—the marriage battle, the lesbian and gay movement should embark on a proactive, aggressive, national campaign to chip away at stereotypes and stymie the political tactics the right wing uses so well against us." She used the following technique: first, she directed the attention of the reader to a scapegoat, the "right wing." She deceptively laid the blame for the rejecting of gay marriage by a majority of Americans on the "right wing stereotypes" rather than place the blame on what she admitted later in the article: She admitted that American society was not ready for gay marriage because of the "the moral and social concerns of many heterosexuals."

She went on to reveal the next deceptive step: "Crucial in this effort would be a change in public school curriculums [sic] to address diversity and prejudice head-on." How can a subculture believe they have a right to force their beliefs on the innocent minds of American children? It is likely that legislators will eventually bend to special interest money and pressure, ignoring the will of the majority of parents. The minds of American children are seen as fertile ground for agendas of many minorities (the environmental movement has been the most successful thus far). Parents' rights are being replaced by preferential treatment in the classroom for the ideas of environmentalists, gays, women's rights, etc. Parents are the caretakers of their children's social attitudes and moral beliefs, not the schools.

Next, Martinac continues, gay leaders should seek to undermine the role of religious institutions to preserve and manifest the moral principles needed to maintain a civil society. These institutions provide one of the few remaining citadels that inspire our higher nature in contrast to our lower nature. According to Martinac, Gays should add to the moral confusion already present in society by causing division between religious leaders. She understands the role of religion to guard morality, but that did not prevent her from advocating gaining "support of mainstream religious leaders, who are the society's appointed guardians of morality."

If Americans accept gay marriage and continue to normalize the gay lifestyle, they will have validated all sexual activity. Without a viable definition as to what is right or wrong sexually, the door will be open to sexual license. For example, even liberals were shocked in the Spring of 1999 when an article in a respected journal of the American Psychological Association claimed that sex with children was not very harmful to most children and could be a positive experience for many. It was an obvious move by pedophiles to normalize sexual child abuse just as psychology had normalized homosexuality by removing it from its diagnostic book, DSM. The Psychological Association at first resisted withdrawing its support from the article, but after pressure from Dr. Laura Schlessinger, many Americans, and some congressional members, it withdrew its support of the scientific accuracy of the article (which was faulty). This was an example of what happens when a society has no clear moral distinctions between right and wrong—anything goes.

Personal Reflections On Gays

When I was a child living in a Southern California beach town, there were many gays who made their homes there. They had certain beaches they frequented. My friends and I knew which beaches were gay beaches, and we didn't go to them. My mother had told me about homosexuals. She worked with many gays in the restaurant business. She had friendly relationships with a number of gay men. She said she could relate to them more easily than other men because they had more in common. My mother's attitude left me with an impression that gays were different but not to be feared.

I have had numerous associations with gay men and lesbians throughout my life. Once, while working as a seamstress in a psychedelic Broadway show, my husband and I became friends with a transvestite performer. He had a very good sense of humor, and we enjoyed his theatrical energy. He was kind and generous. Putting aside his sexual choice, we could appreciate his friendship. These kinds of experiences show that it is possible to disapprove of a person's actions but still accept the person.

Moreover, one of the most supportive teachers I had in high school was rumored to be a lesbian. It was common knowledge around school, although we had no evidence. We did not shun or fear her because she made no show of being a lesbian. She didn't feel the need to win approval for her choice; at school her role was that of a teacher not a lesbian. She didn't confuse her roles. She didn't try to change our cultural ideas or our morals. She kept her private life to herself, and the students respected her and her privacy. Consequently, she was a very effective teacher and guide to many of the students.

There were two other teachers at my high school that were also very influential who had the reputation of being lesbians. The fact that we believed they were lesbians did not undermine their effectiveness as teachers. They were some of the best. Their sexual choices were not thought important to them or us. However, they did not make a show of their sexual preference or demand acceptance. They did not demand that we accept their subculture or try to impose their moral values and life choices on us. They were willing to accept the consequences of their choice to behave socially in a way that placed them outside the norms of mainstream culture. My friends and I respected them for respecting our moral and cultural boundaries and not trespassing those boundaries.

Many gays have recently tried to change society by claiming that their lifestyle is genetically determined and not a choice. As a church counselor, my experience does not confirm that claim (neither does science). I directly counseled a number of gay men and lesbians and helped them change from gay to straight. They have since been able to relate to the opposite sex in a healthy way and have gone on to get married. All of their problems stemmed from their early home life.

I will generalize for a moment to give an example of the kind of circumstances that can push a child towards becoming gay. For men, they can have dominating mothers and absent fathers (there are a number of home scenarios that can set up a child to become gay). A man could have a slight build and a gentle nature. Other children and relatives often impose labels on smaller, more sensitive men. As they hear from others, or in their own minds, the lie that they are gay, they are pulled into the gay subculture. There, as in all subcultures, they feel acceptance and receive positive attention. For the women, there are also different home scenarios that can set them up. They can be large-boned and athletic. They might have failed to receive sufficient affection from their mothers or had a father who wanted them to be a boy. All of these and other dynamics in the home play a part in the choice of a man or woman, boy or girl, becoming gay.

When I say make a choice, I do not mean that most gays believe they have a choice. There is a kind of brainwashing that goes on from early childhood. People make insinuations, and self-doubt and false accusations enter a child's mind. Over time many factors, plus the recent idea that a person is born gay, join together to push a person into believing they are gay. It is my contention that most gays are deceived into accepting a lie that they are gay. Becoming a gay man or lesbian is not usually a conscious choice. Most gays make an unconscious choice based on lies and deceptions formulated in their minds from a young age.

Although there is help for gays to become straight, it is difficult once they have been deeply involved in the subculture. There are deep feelings of shame that can isolate them emotionally from society, and there are some very personal, satisfying aspects to being a homosexual. People in subcultures always find more acceptance within their group. There is a deep bonding when people feel oppressed by the mainstream.

Homosexuality is not new. What is new to our society is the demand by homosexuals that mainstream society accepts their lifestyle as normal. Gays have never before expected and demanded that the morality of the larger culture change for them. It is new for them to claim they are a minority who must be accepted and recognized as a birth minority. It is new to have them push public schools to include the homosexual culture as a part of the multicultural training—learning to accept and appreciate differences.

In education, they have won acceptance by the teachers' unions, and the unions are the most powerful entities in education. At the present, many teachers' associations are more powerful than parents and school boards. Unless Americans wake up to the revolution that is occurring, it is only a matter of time before children will be taught in school that homosexuality is normal, and that each of them needs to find out which they are—gay or straight. The question will not be about choice; it will be about predestination. Children will be told (or taught) that what is false is true and what is wrong is right. The confusion and lies that already rob many young children of a normal life will increase as schools establish homosexuality as normal.

Homosexuals need to respect what is good for the whole society, not just for themselves. They need to restrain themselves from using manipulation, lies, and deception to gain their own selfish ends. Many amendments to the Constitution protect the rights of the few, and gay rights are protected by these amendments because they are American citizens. However, it is wrong for them to deceive the public and to refuse to be responsible for their choices. They have made a choice, and they have to live with the consequences of their choice just as anyone in society has to suffer consequences when they break the moral norms of that society. Since the 1960s, Americans have increasingly sought ways to make choices and avoid the consequences. We have become consistently more irresponsible and have found creative ways to avoid being accountable for our conduct. Gays are a part of this same moral breakdown. If they and others continue to ignore moral laws and principles and demand society change to accommodate their moral beliefs, the society will lose more of the moral principles that preserve community and the common good.

Special Interests Use The Democratic Party

Since the 1960s, feminists, gays, environmentalists, people of color, unions, and liberal educators have aligned themselves with the liberal part of the Democratic Party. Democrats have used government to be a benevolent caretaker of the different special interests rather than public servants who are obligated to consider the common good. Of course, politicians are always obligated to consider their individual constituents, but the common good must always remain a guiding principle in each decision. Beginning with Lyndon Johnson, the Liberals in the Democratic Party asserted their control over the Party after Kennedy's death.

Liberal special interests united and began demanding access and power in the decisions of the Democratic Party. They started to use the media and manipulative techniques to win support. Increasingly, they put their agendas before the will of the majority. They lost sight of the democratic principle promoting the greatest good for the greatest number. Instead, they focused on what was good for their cause rather than the good of the majority. Then as political parties weakened, they put pressure on liberal politicians to support their agendas. The ability of various minority groups to obtain control of the minds and votes of citizens and, more so, the politicians through the use of the media and money, is one of the greatest threats to the United States and to its form of government.

The Founding Fathers set up a democratic, republican form of government in which the majority rule was to be protected by the check and balance of factions. These factions were not destructive as long as they did not unite by compromising their principles. Yet, once liberal groups ignored principle in order to unite with similar factions, they formed an unyielding monopoly of political power. They consciously used the media to solidify their power. They, as did the capitalists, began to manage public opinion. President Jimmy Carter expressed his fears and disappointment in the power of special interests over government and the will of the majority in his "malaise" speech of 1979: "You see Congress twisted and pulled in every direction by hundreds of well-financed and powerful special interests. You see every extreme position defended to the last vote, almost the last breath by one unyielding group or another."[4] Further evidence of the power of special interests is seen in the unhealthy fear of most Americans to express thoughts that are not considered politically correct. All speech about people of color and liberal special interests is closely observed with all seriousness to find any slight or deprecation. Citizens have to be constantly updated on the most recent proper term to use to refer to an ethnic or racial group. People are constantly being criticized and judged for any expression that edges towards criticism of any minority group. The threat of being labeled a racist or a bigot restricts communication between people, causing the needless continuation of ethnic and racial divisions.

A Missed Fork In The Road:
A Summary of Special Interest Influence

With the rise to power of special interests in the 1970s, came intense division. Each special interest put its own concerns above our nation's interests. They cared only for what they saw as their need for their self-ful-fillment. As described above, they were determined to change the culture to fit their needs. They gave into tendencies of their lower nature to become self-absorbed and ruled by emotion. Journalist Mike Weis, San Jose Mercury News, repeated parts of President Carter's malaise speech in 1979. Weis said Carter warned us that we were at a crossroads. He said to follow the right path would take "sacrifice and a common purpose."[5]

Carter further explained: "That path leads to true freedom for our nation and ourselves." We failed to follow that path. The other path, "a path I've warned about tonight…leads to fragmentation and self-interest. Down that road is a mistaken idea of freedom, the right to grasp for ourselves some advantage over others." "That path" he said "would be one of constant conflict between narrow interests ending in chaos and immobility. It is a certain route to failure." President Carter was right.

This self-love and "me first" attitude has led to a dependence upon government that leads to irresponsibility. One of the weaknesses of democracies is that their citizens tend to turn to the government to provide for them. In that situation, the people fail to criticize or hold the government accountable as long as it is providing for their particular needs. Citizens who over-depend on government do not want to see their government's faults or correct them. Consequently, government becomes too powerful and no longer answerable to the people. For example, the National Organization of Women (NOW) refused to criticize Clinton during the Paula Jones lawsuit and the Monica Lewinsky scandal—even though he behaved in a way for which they had criticized every other politician or public official. They used a double standard in order to protect their own interests and agenda. They were not motivated by a desire to promote the common good but their own good. It is this kind of duplicity used by special interest groups, who are the few, that is undermining the will of the many, the majority.

This ongoing self-centeredness, which began in the late 1960s, has caused the increasing divisiveness in American society. Multicultural diversity is constantly put forward as the means to create a unified utopia. We are supposed to accept each other as we learn about each other's differences. The more we have promoted multiculturalism the more we have become divided. It is because every ethnic group, minority, or special interest group puts itself first. These groups can think only of their rights and needs, and do not ask if their goals and/or methods are best for the greatest number.

What will unite America again is the restoration of the knowledge and practice of the public philosophy. This philosophy will reestablish the American culture that was founded on common goals and a common culture. The traditions of civility would help to clarify those things that make Americans one. What do Americans have in common that makes us identify ourselves as Americans—that unites us? The majority of Americans have certain things in common. At some point in history, most Americans' ancestors came from some other place. The immigrants who came here by choice have character qualities in common. They (or their ancestors) have courage, a spirit of adventure, the ambition to better their lives and the lives of their families, a hunger for freedom, a desire to own property, a strong streak of individualism and independence, a belief in the value of hard work, a hope in equal opportunity, and a love for their children. In fact, the love for their children is so strong that immigrants will leave behind family, friends, and safety for a dream of providing a better life for their children. In addition, Americans need to place the importance of good character at the top of their list of values. Then, by restoring these qualities and values, America can restore its oneness and identity.

Many liberals reject the idea of one American culture, but when Americans from an ethnic or racial group return to visit their ancestral homeland, even though they may look the same as the citizens of that country, they are immediately identified as Americans. Americans have a way of talking and thinking that separates them from their previous culture. The American character makes us one; it unites us. It does not matter if we are from Asia, Mexico, Russia, India, or Iran; within two or three generations we look, talk, and act like Americans. We have a mainstream culture that is strong and healthy. All of the subcultures enrich the mainstream, but they cannot replace it. If we all glorify our sub-cultural, racial and ethnic roots instead of our mainstream identity, we will remain divided.

Two racial groups, the Native Americans and the African Americans, have a different initial American experience. At first, they were dominated instead of set free. Although there has been improvement for both races, America has further to go to fulfil its dream of being a "City on a Hill." The treatment of Native American and African American citizens, although improved, does not yet fulfill the original American dream. American society will never be perfectly integrated in body, mind, and spirit; but we must always strive to include everyone in America's identity. The prejudices that arise out of past relationships and new relationships with new immigrants should be a constant reminder of our imperfections and need to continue steadfastly in our efforts "to do justly and to love mercy" ever increasingly.

Native Americans and African Americans are a gift to the American experience and identity. There is a history and heritage of each culture that enriches and balances the American culture. Native Americans remind us to respect nature and to remember that life is more than making money and possessing things. They are a voice of balance, which reminds us that we have a spirit that needs to be fed. African Americans give us an example of the power of suffering to create a loving and compassionate nature. They add the richness of warmth, exuberance, passion, and openness to our American character.

America is a melting pot; we should not be a pot full of marbles banging against each other. The idea of the melting pot has fallen from favor in the last thirty years, but it is a reality recognized and described as early as the 1760s by a French immigrant, Michel Guillaume Jean de Crevecoeur. He saw a "new man" created by the American experience. He extolled the virtues of American diversity and unity when he said: "He is an American, who leaving behind him all his ancient prejudices and manners, receives new ones from the new mode of life he has embraced, the new government he obeys, and the new rank he holds. He becomes an American by being received in the broad lap of our great Alma Mater. Here the individuals of all nations are melted into a new race of men, whose labours and posterity will one day cause great changes in the world...The American is a new man, who acts upon new principles; he must therefore entertain new ideas, and form new opinions. From involuntary idleness, servile dependence, penury, and useless labour, he has passed to toils of a very different sort, rewarded by ample subsistence. This is an American."[6]

The cultural mixture that makes up America is superior to each of its individual parts or subcultures. We need to appreciate what makes Americans one. It is time to come back together, bringing with us our special contributions. By pouring the best attributes of our identities into a common pot, American culture will thrive and continually improve. In order to unite, each subculture must put our country, all of its people and institutions, before their own selfish interests. Individual special interests must be willing to sacrifice some of their individual agendas for the good of the whole. In a democratic republic the few do not have the right to rule the many. It is time to act from our higher nature and restore a United States of America.

Chapter 6.

The Media: Tool for Deception

Media Has Been Used to Change Our Culture

The nineteenth and twentieth century philosophers were not the first philosophers to question God's existence and the ability to know truth. Xenophanes and Protagoras, pre-socratic philosophers, believed man was the central figure in creation and not the gods or a God. Xenophanes thought man created God in his own likeness, and Protagoras made the famous statement that "man is the measure of all things." Philosophers have been trying to solve the mysteries of the universe and discover truth for centuries. Although some of their ideas have always filtered down to the common man, they have not had a life changing effect on people's day-to-day lives, especially on their moral values. Religion has previously been a stronger influence on moral beliefs and acceptable conduct than philosophy.

Many sociologists have theorized on the innumerable causes of the radical change in American culture over the last thirty years. They have grappled with a confusing mesh of causes, not being able to place responsibility on one thing more than any other. Since the source of our cultural demise has been illusive, it has added to the feeling of powerlessness hovering over Americans. Polls tell parents that their children are happy and moral, but those reports do not appease their feelings of unrest. There has been a multiple list of causes: economic abundance, consumerism, more powerful media, psychology, outlawing prayer in school, the Hippie Movement, two parents working, the Civil Rights Movement, and the diminishing influence of the Judeo/Christian moral standards, to mention only a few. The causes for this cultural change appear so numerous that most Americans feel helpless to change it. The only hope for restoring a stable, healthy, civil culture is to focus on the core reason or reasons for the change.

The thesis of this book points to the loss of the public philosophy or the traditions of civility as the source of the cultural revolution. It is its theoretical or philosophical source. Yet, this new culture, which expressed itself outwardly in the Hippie subculture and then liberal left ideas, was not completely new. Many of its tenets had been promoted since America's founding. There have been movements idealizing going back-to-nature and developing communal utopias throughout America's history. The Transcendentalist writings of the 18th century contained many of these ideas. They believed humans were essentially good and filled with boundless potential. The suffrage movement, which fought for the right of women to vote, also included proponents of sexual freedom. However, these beliefs stayed within an elite, intellectual, and celebrity group.

For centuries many writers, as well as artists, idealized and romanticized these lifestyles. Advocates of revolutionary ideas have always tried to win converts. (It is common practice to reduce one's feeling of shame for breaking cultural norms by enticing others into the same wrongdoing.) In America, there has always been an elite group proselytizing for various reforms. Most of them failed to become part of the mainstream mentality. The common man fantasized about these romantic ideas, but the majority did not accept them in practice. Most Americans accepted the public philosophy with its traditions of civility, which were passed on to them by previous generations. They believed in its values, even if they were tempted to follow the others. They were not always successful in living up to these moral ideals, but they considered them the standards one should strive to achieve.

Since the public had resisted conversion to romantic ideas for centuries, how did a cultural revolution occur in the 1960s? What was different in the 1960s and 1970s from other times that caused a cultural revolution? What was different to cause ideas that had been on the fringes of the main culture to now establish dominance? It was the invention, availability, and use of the tools of the technological media—radio, movies, and television. These tools were used to popularize the romantically based liberal culture that has replaced America's public philosophy. Of course, there had already been a weakening of the public philosophy by the "enlightened self-interest" of the industrial philosophies. Yet, if the technological media had not been invented, Romantic ideas would not have been able to transform the self-interest of the industrial philosophy into the self-love of the liberal philosophy so quickly.

The 1960s and 1970s differed from previous times of reform because the generation born in the late 1930s and early 1940s was the first human product of the Information Age. These 1950s teenagers were the first humans to be formed by a combination of movies, television, and radio. They experienced the full power of the communication media without having had any preparation. No one had ever had this media experience before, and therefore, there was no handbook on how to handle its manipulative power. For the first time in the history of humankind, radical thinkers had a unique, magical, mesmerizing tool to promote non-mainstream ideas. This power became a dynamic tool for planned control by various special interests with their philosophical viewpoints. Much of the media influence was used to promote capitalist goals and liberal, minority causes. Without the guidance of the public philosophy, the majority was swallowed up by manipulative symbols and images. This new media element, never seen before historically, has been the Pandora's Box of the twentieth century.

It has not been the violence and sex in the entertainment media by themselves that have had power. It has been the ideas behind the use of the images that have been mind altering. Anyone who saw the 1999 movie

"Pleasantville" could ascertain its purpose was to influence sexual behavior. Those who made the film intended to promote free love or sex outside of marriage. They used the image of black and white film in contrast to colored film to show the difference between those who had traditional sexual values and those who believed in sexual freedom. The controlled, lifeless, self-righteous people of the fifties were shown in black and white, while the bright, free people of the nineties were shown in color. When two young people in the nineties went back in time to the fifties, they brought the nineties sexual practices with them. They touched people's lives with their sexually free behavior and ideas. As those they influenced cast off their sexual inhibitions, they turned from black and white to color. Free sex was romanticized by contrasting the colorful world of those who had changed with the black and white world of the stodgy, rigid traditionalists who refused to change. This movie was intended to be a propaganda film; it was not intended to be a work of art.

Psychology And The Media

Added to the power of the media was the birth of psychology in the late nineteenth century. The research in psychology has provided tools, unknown previously, to control and manipulate the mind. Most Americans in my era heard about the experiment with Pavlov's dogs. Pavlov trained them to do what he wanted through the use of pain and pleasure. These kinds of psychological discoveries enhanced the use of mind control. Since the advent of psychology, politicians, revolutionaries, intellectuals, the licentious, and powerbrokers have discovered the vulnerability of the subconscious to certain primordial and emotion-causing symbols. As the century has progressed, those who have sought power have become more adept at manipulating and controlling the minds of the public, turning the public into the masses.

Individuals or groups have used the psychological tool of manipulation to hide their real intentions or motives. Since formal authority in the American government has rested with the people and not with a group or person, those in positions of power have had a choice to educate and persuade the public or to trick and manipulate them to support their objectives. The temptation to use the immense power of the modern media has overwhelmed the moral resolve of most factions and individuals wanting more authority. Their consciences have had little power to restrain their deceptive practices since the loss of the public philosophy. C. Wright Mills explains the difference between use of legitimate authority and manipulation: "Authority is power that is explicit and more or less 'voluntarily' obeyed; manipulation is the 'secret' exercise of power, unknown to those who are influenced."[1]

The consumer economy was the first obvious consequence of using psychology and the media. Corporations developed commercials using various symbols to play on human desires and emotions. In spite of the negative aspects of the consumer economy, it has not been the use of marketing commercials that has caused our present moral decay and cultural revolution. The increase in the impulse to buy and the excesses of materialism have been a distraction to righteous living, but they have not been the cause of the loss of moral standards and the corrosion of the conscience. The true culprits have been individuals and groups who previously could only attract a minority of support from the public. Since the 1960s, they have chosen to use the media to deceive and seduce the public to accept their ideas and agendas. They have increasingly improved their techniques of mind control and manipulation to blind and mesmerize the majority of Americans.

Manipulative techniques have improved and expanded through the years. Numerous lessons were learned about how to use the media during World War II when it was used to gain support for the war effort. These ideas were further developed to increase consumerism after the War. Advertising experts found ways to manipulate the public. They used symbols in commercials to play on a person's imagined identity. People could imagine themselves to be a different person if they drove a certain car, wore a specific cologne or perfume, wore a certain kind of clothes, etc. "Madison Avenue" found that people were very vulnerable to images and symbols that defined them. Then, the methods used to turn American citizens into consumers were adapted to political and special interest causes. Corporations began to use the media to convey capitalist, free market ideas. Commercials were used to create the image that corporate freedom and individual freedom were complementary.

At the present time, conservatives and liberals play on opposing desires in Americans—the desire for individuality, independence, and freedom and the desire for security and for escape from freedom. Symbols are used to appeal to these deeply imbedded desires and feelings. When emotions are subtly played upon, they prevent the public from truly evaluating and reflecting upon the practices and goals of corporate or liberal special interests. They respond to symbols, not reasonable ideas. Other methods of manipulation are lies, exaggerations, distractions, half-truths, fear, false-accusations, condemnation, repetition, and name-calling. One of the favorite names to call an opponent who is outside of the two political parties or who is attacking the status quo is, crank or crackpot. It only takes one of these labels to cause the American public to write off a credible candidate or patriot. How can a person prove they are not a crackpot to millions of people if the media does not air their defense?

A perfect example of the use of distraction and half-truths to deceive the public happened when Clinton and some politicians responded to the massacre at Columbine High School. Immediately after the shootings, with the reports of the hardened consciences of the two killers, many people said there was something wrong with morality in America. Immediately, in a flash, the minds of the American people were deceptively distracted to alternative causes: guns, videos, etc. Clinton went on television to redirect the attention of Americans to gun control, making it difficult for people to see past the half-truth that improving some of the gun control laws were justified. The public did not understand that the focus upon the gun issue was a ploy. The intentions of Clinton and his supporters were to keep people's minds off of the real problem, failed character development and morally, uninformed consciences. They did not want people to focus on the present ethical dilemma in American society.

There is a poem I wrote some years back in which I described the manipulation process in the consumer economy. A part of this poem can provide some imagery to help clarify how deception works. I would not put as much emphasis on the consumer part as I did then. Rather, I think the actual method of deception is more important.

> The hand of deception
> -slippery slide-
> Now you see it
> Oops!
> Now you don't.
> Consumer economy
> Buy! Buy! Buy!
> Comfort=happiness, comfort=happiness!
> Buy! Buy! Buy!
> Keep them buying
> Wanting more
> -slippery slide-
> Now you see it,
> Hand of deception,
> Oops!
> Now you don't

When Clinton and other politicians made guns the focal point for reform and legislation, they were actually creating a lie. The lie was to point to guns and the National Rifle Association (NRA) as the evildoers. They played on the need of people to feel secure by giving them an immediate answer to a problem. In the short term, it felt like political leaders were removing the cause for public confusion. Actually, they were adding to the long-term confusion of Americans by directing their attention to a symptom of the disease rather than the cure. When the public allows their minds to be diverted to the branches of a problem, then the root cause remains hidden. The branches will reappear later when the short-term solution runs its course.

Americans could have avoided control of their minds in the Columbine tragedy. They could have avoided being controlled by choosing to want to know the truth and by staying focused on the root cause of the problem. They should have supported the leaders and politicians who kept speaking the truth. The majority knew at a 'gut' level what the real problem was. The majority knew that the cause for the sociopathic behavior of the boys at Columbine in 1999 and the other mass killings by children since 1997 had to be more than a problem of gun control. People knew deep within that our society was in moral trouble.

The testimony of Darrell Scott, father of Rachel Joy Scott, who was killed in the shooting at Littleton, Colorado, confirmed that the root cause for the Columbine tragedy was deeper than gun control, movies, or video games. He made a plea for Congress to look for the core reason behind the killing of his daughter and the ten others. On May 22, 1999 he spoke to the House Judiciary Committee.

The death of my wonderful daughter, Rachel Joy Scott, and the deaths of the heroic teacher and the other children who died, must not be in vain. Their blood cries out for answers. The first recorded act of violence was when Cain slew his brother Abel out in the field. The villain was not the club he used. Neither was it the NCA, the National Club Association. The true killer was Cain, and the reason for the murder could only be found in Cain's heart.

In the days that followed the Columbine tragedy, I was amazed at how quickly fingers began to be pointed at groups such as the NRA. I am not a member of the NRA. I am not a hunter. I do not even own a gun. I am not here to represent or defend the NRA because I don't believe that they are responsible for my daughter's death...I am here today to declare that Columbine was not just a tragedy; it was a spiritual event that should be forcing us to look at where the real blame lies...The real villain lies with our own hearts...

Personal Reflections On Deception

In the 1970s, I was a member of a Christian church in which the pastor was a skillful deceiver. I do not think he was always conscious of the techniques he was using. In that way, he was not unique from other charismatic leaders. Many charming leaders have beguiled people just by the natural expression of their charisma. However, many have also studied these deceptive methods. I think there are a considerable number of government leaders and their staff members who have studied these techniques in recent years. There are authors that have used psychological insights and personal observations of human nature to explain how to play games with people's minds. The modern political consultants are very savvy about human nature and the human psyche.

I will describe the deceptive behavior I experienced in my church in order to shine some light on the deception and manipulation we encounter daily in the media. This Church was formed in the early 1970s; it was part of what was called the Jesus Movement. Many Hippies went off to the country in search of spiritual answers to their confusion about American society. Many of these Hippies and other lost young people were converted by Christian outreach ministries. Since many of them were living communally or essentially homeless, these Christian outreach groups created Christian communities and fellowship groups. Many strong, charismatic pastors or apostles, as some of them preferred to call themselves, rose up out of the need for leadership. Many of them were young and inexperienced Christians themselves and stepped into a difficult and dangerous role. Many of them became overbearing and controlling. These groups existed at the same times as Jim Jones's ministry.

My former husband and I joined one of these fellowships. The pastor was young in years and spiritually immature. He had placed himself in ministry before he was ready. Consequently, the presence of a strong ego or self caused him to dominate his congregation rather than lead them. For example, one time the pastor told all of the church members that we were all equal, and if anyone saw a fault in him, they should feel free to point it out to him. I naively took him at his word, and I went to him about a fault. He had a need to be the center of attention, even when someone else was supposed to be leading songs or teaching. I diplomatically tried to point out to him how he would always push himself forward and steal the show from whoever was in charge in a meeting. His actions were interfering with other members gaining confidence and learning how to minister.

After I described this fault, he immediately and defensively, without a moment's reflection, denied any possibility of erring. He felt I was assaulting him out of wrong motives. His feelings of martyrdom immediately came to the surface. Rather than listen humbly and try to discern if I was right, he immediately called in another elder, who was not yet twenty years old, to tell me how wrong I was. This elder defended the pastor. I knew he and the other elders felt the competition from the pastor, but they had their own ambitions to be leaders and would not confirm my criticisms. They were blinded to his faults because of their own aspirations.

From that moment on I was distrusted by him and all of the elders and elder sisters (women with some authority). In which case, he tried to hold back any influence I might have. He tried to drive a wedge between my husband and I by encouraging my husband to be more dominating. He looked for any fault in me and sent other members to criticize me and question my motives. He slandered me behind my back and sometimes preached sermons that were obviously directed at me. In order to weaken my confidence and identity, he told me my education and spiritual training were a deficit to pleasing God. Amidst all of the attacks, his strongest and most effective tool was shame. He shamed me in front of others a number of times. His main goal was to undermine my confidence in order to make me submissive to his will.

The tools for deception and control were all present in this unique church situation. Hearsay and the gossip chain were like the media. There was a party line of thinking. Everyone was told what the rules were to belong to this "righteous" organization. You had to be loyal to the leader, believe in submission to authority, doubt your own ability to discern the truth, feel ashamed if you did not submit to the will of the elders, and side with the pastor against others when called upon. You could be an accuser one time and the accused the next, so everyone feared everyone else. Suspicion reigned. Whenever someone stepped out of line, the gossip chain went into action to get that person back into line. If someone was disloyal, they were separated or sent out from the rest.

All charismatic leaders have similar qualities. They have a personal leadership style that uses charm and popularity to win support. They have extensive intellectual knowledge. Dynamic leaders have a strong sense of their own power and ability, exuding an unrealistic confidence. They are visionaries with childlike and attractive emotional outbursts and enthusiastic plans. They appear to care about people. They hunger for attention. The weaknesses of these dynamic leaders cause turmoil and division. They usually lack self-control, act on impulse and intuition, depend on charm and deception instead of substance to gain power. This charm often leads to flirtation and sexual involvement with the opposite sex. They reject all criticism as a personal attack, throwing up paranoid defenses. They demand absolute loyalty, harboring secret feelings of suspicion and martyrdom.

For charismatic individuals to become good and effective leaders they have to develop integrity, compassion, diligence, courage, dependability, decisiveness, organizational skills, and self-control. They have to overcome their need to be liked and praised. When manipulation is used by charismatic leaders, those under their spell are easily victimized. Most popular, charismatic leaders are self-protective and unable to take criticism. They see those around them and their critics as competitors who are looking for an opportunity to weaken their authority. There is always an aspect of paranoia in a self-aggrandizing leader, such as with Richard Nixon with Watergate and Jim Jones at Guyana and Clinton in the Lewinsky scandal. This kind of ruler will have a loyal following who remain in favor as long as they blindly agree with the leader's decisions. These individuals will go out and do battle, making all efforts to break down and undermine critics. Since the leader they are defending is supposedly innocent or is promoting a worthy goal, they believe using any means is all right for the good of the leader and the cause.

People are only vulnerable to be controlled by charismatic leaders or by the seduction of the media when they are confused and feel powerless to solve the problems facing them and/or they do not want to be responsible. At those times, humans go into denial and avoid reality. When people are fearful, lazy, and/or insecure they search for someone to provide answers and solutions. They want a savior. Then, they become easy prey for the seductive and deceptive methods of charismatic leaders or emotionally united special interests. Since the 1960s the citizens of the United States have increasingly slipped into denial. Once the liberals and conservatives abandoned the public philosophy, the public let politicians, businessmen, and liberals rule the country. Americans have let their wills and desires be distracted to material interests and have therefore failed to guard their freedom and their souls.

The Tools Of Deception In Politics

How were the tools of deception in my church similar to the use of the media in this country over the last 40 years? As we have seen, there are two different philosophies that have been heavily vying for influence over the last forty years. The capitalists have had their media sources: journalists, radio talk show hosts, spokespersons, certain movies, and television news programs. Although the media has leaned to the left, liberals no longer question certain corporate ideas. Moreover, corporations have gained most of their support through supplying the employment of millions of people. The corporate philosophy has transmitted its greatest influence through the role of the corporations as employers. The corporate philosophy has been second nature and unconsciously integrated into the American worldview.

Presently, since the corporate philosophy is so integrated into American consciousness, the corporate ideas are more subtly expressed than the liberal ones. Although neither feel any shame about using whatever propaganda is necessary to accomplish their objectives, liberals are more obvious in their use of the deceptive methods. As in my church, there are a list of expected liberal beliefs that must be espoused, and a language that must be followed. Liberalism has become a religion with a religious doctrine. Liberals are ever vigilant to band together and close ranks against anyone or any group that thinks differently or conservatively. Attacks by Conservative extremists have intensified the unquestioning support of liberal activists for their leaders. These attacks by Conservatives have generated feelings of suspicion and paranoia.

Moreover, the liberal faithful loyally defend liberal leaders, whether or not they are moral or upright. Their desire for power, which they use for their perceived good purposes, is overly passionate and commends them to misplaced loyalties. They manipulate the public through the media (the gossip chain) in order to promote, protect, and defend their various agendas. They use the powerful tool of shame to promote their goals. Liberals send out spokespersons to call their opponents names, and they feel justified to lie about anything or anyone that interferes with achieving their end. The self-righteousness of liberals reveals the religious nature of their belief-system. The Clinton-Lewinsky scandal is one of the clearest examples of liberal manipulation using the media.

Capitalist manipulation is not dead, either. Microsoft, secretly funding an institute to run so-called 'independent ads,' is a recent example of corporate manipulation. The Independent Institute ran ads in newspapers to support Microsoft's case in the antitrust trial initiated by the federal government. An article by Joel Brinkley in the New York Times and reproduced in the San Jose Mercury News reported that "the Independent Institute made an extraordinary effort to portray itself as beholden to no one…Throughout the trial, it has often taken Microsoft's side."[2] The Institute put out a full-page ad in the New York Times in which 240 academic experts signed on to support Microsoft's case. Microsoft deceived people into thinking that this Institute was acting independently. It was just one more incident of unethical means being used by a capitalist to preserve his power.

Furthermore, the article referred to an economic ideology espoused by economic academics called the "Chicago School, which holds that, in general, government should not enforce antitrust laws. The theory holds that market forces will destroy an inefficient monopoly, but an efficient monopoly, while impervious to competitors, provides consumers all the benefits of competition."[3] It is just another version of the survival of the fittest, laissez-faire philosophy and enlightened self-interest. These ideologues are saying that corporations do not need to be regulated because competition in the free market will cause those corporations to survive who provide the most service to the public at the cheapest price. As corporations pursue their self-interest, the free market will protect the interest of employees and consumers. Not surprisingly, reality does not bear out this theory. Many employees of global corporations are presently treated as little more than slave laborers. Moreover, once a monopoly is efficient, there is no guarantee they will pass on any savings to consumers. There is no sign that human nature has become altruistic in the last thirty years, causing corporations, of their own free will, to put the general good before profit. It is the same industrial propaganda that has been seducing the public since the Industrial Revolution. It is only in a slightly different package

The Specific Corporate And Liberal Ideas Promoted Through The Media

The corporate or industrial belief system has its beginnings in the Industrial Revolution. All Americans in the twentieth century have been raised with free market, capitalist ideals. They have learned to accept this belief system without reflection: The following is common capitalist propaganda: "a) Anything wrong in our society is a problem, amenable to a solution in the interest of all, b) We'll all be best off if business manages the development of resources in the future. c) It can do this only if (a) profits are high and (b) there is a minimum of government interference. d) Solutions to problems are generally technical; we need new technology, but not any change in the system e) Hence, what the experts decide is best for all. The people are often deficient in understanding. f) However, neither business nor technocrats have much power; in the present system, the people are the ones who decide. g) They decide best through individual purchases in a free market; voting is secondary, and other kinds of politics are a potential threat to free choice. h) Growth and productivity are good for all. I) Our needs— for pleasure, love, approval, security, etc.—can best be met by consuming products. j) Consumption should generally be done by units no larger than the nuclear family. And the nuclear family is the social ideal."4

A few other "corporate truths" could be added: a) Happiness is having a good paying job that provides for the good life. b) It is a threat to the economy for wages to rise too high. Therefore, corporations need to hold down wages and hire contractors to avoid inflation. c) Both parents should work to provide for all of the needs of the family, especially to provide the higher education their children will need to obtain high-paying corporate jobs. d) Capitalism and democracy are nearly the same thing, and one cannot exist without the other.

The liberal belief systems has its history in Romantic ideas, labor, progressives, New Deal, big government, free love, feminists, people of color, environmentalists, and recently, global economy. It is very different from the corporate one, but there are now some crossovers that will be stated at the end of the list. a) Government should be used for the good of the people. b) Liberals are the good guys who care about the underprivileged, people of color, the environment, laborers, and educating our children. c) Most parents are failing to raise their children with the right attitudes and values. d) Therefore, liberal government should be involved in raising and training children. e) Those liberals in power know best what the people need, but the people still rule. f) Liberals can use the media deceptively to obtain public support because they know what is best for them. g) The check and balance system of our forefathers is outmoded because it makes it difficult to pass important legislation. h) Happiness is having a good job and experiencing self-fulfillment and self-esteem. i) It is all right for both parents to work as long as government can provide exceptional child and day care services. The village can be used to raise the children. j) Liberals preserve the superior, multicultural heritage of immigrants, and different cultures should not melt into mainstream culture. k) Liberals should use government and education to create the just society and promote human goodness, which is attainable through careful monitoring and planning.

Some liberals are moving to the right on these issues: l) The free market provides the most abundance for all. m) Through global unity nations shall lessen in power and importance. n) Global economy is good for the people of America. n) Government should help American corporations expand overseas.

Liberals and Conservatives
Could Have Used Noble Means

The women's movement, people of color, environmentalists, and liberal educators did not need to undermine the public philosophy to promote their causes. The principles to support many of their issues could be found in the public philosophy. The standards for justice and fairness exist in the Judeo-Christian principles and the natural law. For example, the revelation from Scriptures about the priesthood of all believers, expounded by Martin Luther, was one of the main factors convincing philosophers that the masses could become a ruling public. This idea gave each individual a new importance. Since all humans could be believers, were equal before God, and could come before God without an intermediary; it made all believers—men, women, children, slaves, and people of color—equally important. No group of people or race could any longer be considered superior by birth to any other human being.

Many of the obstacles against women's rights are a residue from centuries of cultural and religious interpretations of the role of women in society. Rather than create a permanent wall of separation between religion and modern women, feminists could have promoted a healthy public debate to apply intellectual scholarship to church doctrines about women. Many passages in the Scriptures can be seen in a cultural context. Many limitations on women's rights in America have been the result of interpretations of certain Scriptural passages. These passages could have been seen in their cultural context. Some controversial passages about women could have been reevaluated by comparing the cultural setting of Jesus' time with the cultural setting of today. These debates would in time have led to more acceptance of women in business, politics, and church government without throwing away the positive value given to women by Judeo-Christian doctrines.

All of the liberal special interest groups, except gays, could have stood on various natural law principles and Christian Judeo-Christian principles, just as King used the concept of "agape," godly, unconditional love, to support the Civil Right's Movement. From the center of his Christian faith King clung to the belief that "God was on the side of truth and justice."[5] He also contended that even if people did not believe in a God, they must see that "the universe is on the side of justice."[6] The Civil Rights movement was based on Judeo-Christian beliefs, natural laws, and principles of civil disobedience. Other liberal, special interests could have turned to the same traditional value system that had inspired all noble American movements. Instead, they were impatient, and the media was available to follow a quicker and easier path

Other Common Means Of Deception

Americans are asleep. They must wake up from the deception imposed upon their minds. Slowly, since the beginning of the Cold War, an increasing number of Americans have not wanted to know the truth. Choosing to be responsible became difficult as their seemed to be no answers to international problems. During the first years of the Cold War, and into the 1960s, there was the feeling that nuclear war with the Soviet Union was inevitable. People were talking about preparing shelters for a nuclear holocaust while believing that nothing could really save them. With this kind of reality, fantasy or denial seemed the only means to keep from becoming depressed or going insane. In addition, with the assassinations of the John and Bobby Kennedy and King in the 1960s, Americans could not help but withdraw in order to heal from the terrible loss and trauma caused by the deaths of their greatly loved leaders. The period of shock and mourning has extended over many years, leaving our nation with fewer high-quality leaders.

Americans have given over their self-rule to leaders who are as lost as themselves, but these leaders have put their selfish goals before the common good. Without a well-informed and alert public, those desiring influence have used this time to move into power. As mentioned above, they have developed methods of mind-control. There are many ways to control people's minds. We have already observed the technique of distracting people from a serious problem by focusing their attention upon lesser problems or upon solutions based upon half-truths. In addition, loyal followers of a charismatic leader or a highly emotional special interest unite in a mixture of mutual ambition and self-deception to throw up screens of lies that sound reasonable. Also, those close to powerful people fear the very power they desire. This fear keeps them in the fold. Finally, using shame and destroying reputations with lies and slander is a very successful tool. In all of these cases, the use of the media makes these methods extremely successful.

There are other methods not yet mentioned. Politicians send out spokespersons to repeat the same message endlessly to make the public accept the information as a fact. The Network News leaves out some of the facts of a story or spends little time reporting on subjects unfavorable to their corporate ties or to their liberal beliefs. The public is made to feel others know more than it does about foreign policy, the schools, and government, causing citizens to depend on experts to tell them how to think. Citizens are made to feel fearful about their economic well being, keeping them from looking at the bad policies and the poor character of their leaders.

More often than not politicians tell the public how to think rather than ask for their direction. Since I am in education, I see this sheep mentality constantly. Recently I went to a conference in which all school board members and superintendents had to express their opinions about how we should teach our children. Educational thinkers and professors from the most recent educational ideology created everything that was spoken. It was amazing to see everyone there adapt to a change in ideology without even questioning how they could accept something they spent years criticizing. The usual jargon was expressed: learning to learn, life-long learning, cooperative learning, teamwork, and hands-on learning. However, out of every mouth came words hated, despised, and fought against for thirty years. Every participant agreed we needed to teach children "the basics"— reading, writing, and math.

Surprisingly, everyone there appeared to accept this new dogma without questioning. No one asked themselves why they had been told to reject "the basics" all these years if they were right. No one complained that they had been misled and now had to embrace something they were told was boring and unnecessary. Everyone just accepted the "new" idea passively and enthusiastically as if they had just come up with a great idea. These are the same people who are insisting our children need to be taught how to think critically. How will educators trained in a non-questioning atmosphere be able to teach their students how to think critically? They have been taught to accept educational ideas as if the gods had handed them down from heaven.

In education, as in other professions, people have been told that in this Information Age there is too much knowledge for every person to learn. Individuals can know only a limited amount of information. Teachers have been told it is the teacher's job to teach, not create the best methods for teaching. In fact, they have been told that they do not know the best methods to use for teaching. Consequently, an elite group of professional educators create and transmit to teachers the so-called "best practices" for teaching. Teachers have been brainwashed to believe that others know better than they do. I am certain that many of them feel an urge to deny and resist most of the theories they are taught, but most teachers do not resist the pressure to conform. Fearing criticism from administrators and undervaluing their own knowledge and expertise, most teachers passively accept the constant stream of new educational fads.

Teachers are not the only ones to doubt their abilities to have a broad range of knowledge. Citizens feel the same inadequacy in making political and governmental decisions. The news media holds back information that the public needs to know in order to be able to govern. They are made to feel they cannot grasp all of the information needed to make a wise decision. For example, there is an idea that information in the Information Age has become so voluminous that no one can learn this information. Therefore, individuals, having limited knowledge, must depend on others to tell them what is best for them and the country. Knowledge passed on for thousands of years is thought of as outdated.

Propaganda makes people forget that wisdom and understanding do not depend upon information alone. Information is factual; it is a small part of knowledge and understanding. Knowledge builds one layer of facts and ideas upon another. As a person learns, learning becomes easier. New connections in the brain are made quickly as layers multiply. Then, understanding and insights spring out of these connections. All knowledge has a relationship to other knowledge. Principles learned in math apply to English; principles learned in philosophy apply to physics; principles learned in psychology relate to history; and the principles from all disciplines become interrelated. When experience is added to the mixture, wisdom and common sense are the result. In that case, new information is not overwhelming. A person can decipher what is important to add to the network of understanding and what to exclude. That is why the saying by Ecclesiastes that "There is nothing new under the sun" will always remain true. There is nothing new of any great importance under the sun. Information has little importance without fitting into a larger system of knowledge.

How Can Americans Escape
Manipulation By Use Of The Media?

At this point in our study of the media and deception, we need a plan to extricate Americans from the seductive and deceptive ideas and feelings that cover their minds. We know that economic conservatives and liberals have unethically manipulated the public by using the communication media. I could go on listing all of the tricks politicians, psychologists, and consultants have found to control people's minds, which would be too numerous to fully comprehend. No one could ever remember all of them every moment in order to assure freedom from control. In a more helpful manner, I will describe one personal decision each individual can make, enabling them to see through the manipulation and deception.

To take the first step to gain freedom, individual Americans need to acknowledge that they have been manipulated into losing their freedom. In addition, they have also chosen to be irresponsible and to give up their freedom. They have not wanted to know the truth or make decisions. Life has appeared too overwhelming since World War II. In some ways it was, but now we can remove ourselves from the subjective confusion of the past and objectively decide how to restore civility and duty to our nation. I learned from my choices in the Christian cult that I was responsible for turning over my will to another person. I needed to take responsibility for my choice and choose to be responsible for my life and my decisions. So too, individual Americans need to choose to be responsible citizens. Then their eyes will be open to the manipulation they presently cannot see. The veil of deception will fall off people's minds when they choose to know the truth. The following is what each American must choose to do to restore self-rule:

- Americans must choose to know the truth even though they fear knowing it.

- Americans must choose to know the truth even though the truth is painful. The truth often hurts, but the truth sets you free.
- Americans must choose to know the truth even though they do not want the responsibility that comes with knowing it.
- Americans must choose to know the truth even though the lazy part of their nature wants to take the easy way.
- Americans must choose to know the truth even though they like the pleasure that comes from following instincts and impulses. They must become disciplined and assert self-control.
- Americans must choose to know the truth in order to take back control of their lives and their government.
- Americans must believe that they possess the wisdom and the political institutions necessary to solve the problems facing our nation.

It will take courage and maturity for Americans to choose to know the truth. What is the truth? The truth is that Americans have allowed themselves to give up the traditions of civility—the public philosophy—which were the threads that held the fabric of society together.

Without the traditions of civility, humans are little more than animals or children. They are easily duped and become pawns of those who are evil or power-hungry. Without the traditions of civility, Americans cannot be good enough or knowledgeable enough to keep their democratic institutions alive. The traditions of civility call people to replace self-interest and self-love with a sense of duty and a love for others. Having the qualities of compassion, love, courage, responsibility, respect, honesty, trustworthiness, and forgiveness will make Americans good family members, good neighbors, and good citizens.

Once Americans restore the traditions of civility their eyes will be open to the political and legislative changes that need to occur, and they will be able to recognize the politicians who put the general good above personal gain, unrealistic ideas, or special interests. The public philosophy is the only philosophy that can preserve the United States of America as a democratic republic, restoring rule to the people.

How Americans Can Practically Restore Their Rule

Practically, Americans must use the media, including the Internet, to enlarge the source of their knowledge. Only by seeking multiple sources of the news can they piece together the truth about each political news story. At present, liberals have especially found ways to make their agenda appear appealing and to pressure for its acceptance. They play on emotions; thereby disarming the power of reason. Americans will only see through the veil of deception by questioning what they hear and inquiring into the loyalties of those providing the information. There are no individual experts when it comes to political decisions. The Founding Fathers believed that the majority, the public, was the safest depositor of political power. They asserted that collectively the people possessed, after a period of factional compromises and party dissension, the common sense, goodness, and wisdom to make the best political decisions. Do not believe anyone who tells you that citizens need to let special interests tell them how to rule. According to the Founding Fathers, the majority is the safest and best ruler for any nation.

Americans have forgotten how their government works. Voters must remember that elected representatives are the instruments and servants of the people and need to be held accountable. Most of the time public servants are supposed to do the will of the majority. There are times, though, that a representative has to take a moral stand that could be contrary to the desire of the majority. This situation does not occur very often. Generally, when officeholders express the will of the majority, they are instituting those laws that will be most beneficial to the general good. If special interests unite in order to possess power, and elected representatives are a part of these united entities, we will have (and already do have) an oligarchy, not a democracy.

Americans must remember that unity is not always a good thing. Some unity, such as total political unity, which fuses factions, is the death of a democratic republic that is based on check and balance principles. Excessive uniting of factions excludes the people from making political decisions. In that case, special interests separate themselves from the voice of the people, influencing government to do what is best for them or what they think is best for the country. For example, if a school board, the educational unions, and a superintendent over-collaborate, and are in agreement on all issues, having compromised their principles to reach agreement, then there will be no check on the power of any one of them. They will achieve power that is independent from the people and hidden from public scrutiny (cloakroom politics). Decisions will be made behind the scenes rather than in public. To put a stop to this practice, citizens need to return to seeking power through their representatives, rather than creating special interest lobbies. The people have to vote out of office those representatives who do not institute their will. They have to observe the actions and decisions of their representatives and hold them accountable to represent their interests not special interests.

Being a good citizen takes observation, study, critical thinking, and involvement. Once individual Americans choose to be responsible, they must fulfill their practical duty to be informed, active citizens. Such actions will restore a sense of power to the majority and free the people from the malaise of impotence.

Chapter 7.

Liberal Education Has Undermined the Public Philosophy

The public educational system is a close second to the power of the media as a tool to change American culture. It has been successfully and consciously used by the corporate and liberal elite to promote their philosophies. In the early days of our republic, education was seen as the major way to preserve and maintain it. Education was a treasure box containing the historical lessons all children needed to know to be good citizens. It contained the knowledge of the traditions of civility, which were the glue to hold the many states and people together. It contained the natural law principles out of which the Declaration of Independence was born, and it contained the knowledge of the Constitution and the principles upon which it was constructed. Public education was seen as the main way to pass on the public philosophy. It was seen by the Founding Fathers as the key to having a republican form of government in which the people ultimately ruled.

The Purpose Of Education
In Our Nation's Beginnings

Education has always been of highest importance to Americans. The Christian settlers were determined that their children would learn to read so they could study the Holy Scriptures. "In the priesthood of all believers, there was no room for illiterates."[1] New England created grammar schools and the schools of higher education, Harvard and Yale, for the sake of imparting a liberal arts education to their children. For the New England settlers there was no separation between religion and secular learning. They were intermingled in order that knowledge would not corrupt character.

Our Founding Fathers and early educators were very aware of the need to give knowledge to the people. James Madison felt much pleasure in the enlightened patriotism of Kentucky "which is now providing for the State a Plan of Education embracing every class of Citizens, and every grade & department of Knowledge."[2] Once the Constitution was written and the republic was established, he and the other founders were active in creating the institutions to maintain it. Madison understood that "A popular Government, without popular information, or the means of acquiring it, is but a Prologue to a Farce or a Tragedy; or, perhaps both. Knowledge will forever govern ignorance: And a people who mean to be their own Governors, must arm themselves with the power which knowledge gives."[3]

Jefferson equally insisted upon education for the masses of people, but he sought to create more of a separation of religion from secular knowledge. He stressed the importance of history over religion in the creation of a knowledgeable public. He wanted students, as future voting public, to have knowledge of the mistakes made by governments and rulers of the past. He was not against the teaching of religion as much as he was against the teaching of religion intermingled with secular studies. Moreover, there was the problem of accommodating all of the various religious sects in each class. Instead, he concluded that there should be separate classes on the university campuses to allow for religious studies. He agreed with those who saw "advantages of associating other studies with those of religion, to establish their religious schools on the confines of the University, so as to give to their students ready and convenient access and…to attend religious exercises with the professor of their particular sect,…"[4]

In spite of the fact that Jefferson preferred to separate secular and religious studies, he did not support excluding moral teaching and character building from schools. None of the Founding Fathers would have considered morality as separate from the study of literature, philosophy, or history. These subjects contained the principles for moral and ethical training in good character. Imparting virtue and the traditions of civil conduct was considered a necessary and integral part of the curriculum. "The ultimate result of the whole scheme of education would be the teaching of all the children of the State reading, writing, and common arithmetic;... The first elements of morality too may be instilled into their minds; such as, when further developed as their judgments advance in strength, may teach them how to work out their greatest happiness by showing them that it does not depend on the condition of life in which chance has placed them, but is always the result of a good conscience, good health, occupation, and freedom in all pursuits."[5]

Americans' belief in education has always been and continues to be (although waning) a secular article of faith. It has been a powerful tradition in the collective memory of Americans, going back to its first colonists. "The Protestant emphasis on education as a means of making God's Word accessible to every Christian merged with the republican notion of education for citizenship and the Enlightenment idea that education would result in the refinement of the individual's rational faculties, the development of science, and the progressive improvement of the race."[6] Education was the answer to every problem, the means by which immigrants became Americans, and it gave hope for a better life and character to all of its participants.

The Effects Of The Industrial Revolution On Education

After the Civil War, industry became a dominant force in American life. As mentioned above, capitalism was on the rise with all of its industrial philosophies developed to support its purposes. The power of industry grew rapidly, transforming America from an agrarian to an urban, industrial society. Of course, education could not avoid being influenced by this change. Reading, writing, and arithmetic continued to be taught in grammar school, but the purpose of education became economic rather than political (educating for citizenship). Good character was still taught, but it shifted to placing more value on the qualities of hard work, independence, loyalty, and enlightened self-interest with less value on the Golden Rule and the qualities of unselfishness and virtue.

Institutions of Higher Learning:

Higher Education went in two different directions. Harvard in the late nineteenth century "grew in company with, and, in general, in harmony with, capitalism."[7] It and most institutions of higher learning were supported by the rich industrialists of the times like Andrew Carnegie. The end of education increasingly became economic rather than a tool for the political and character training of citizens. Although, during the nineteenth century, the faculty remained socially and politically conservative in their attitudes, in the twentieth century, the economic conservative belief system of capitalism began to dominate over civil conservatism.

A second kind of university was formed at the end of the nineteenth century. John Hopkins University in Baltimore was a prototype of the new, progressive view of education. "Sociology, the study of society, gradually made its way into curriculum of the more progressive institutions."[8] This curriculum, based more upon the scientific method, replaced classical learning in these universities and later in all universities. These new universities were less dependent on endowments from businessmen. Faculty members were not required to reflect the economic views of industrialists. They had more opportunity to convey information about the social injustices in the new capitalist society. A student of John Hopkins, Frederick Howe learned "that the industrial system was not what I had assumed it to be in Meadville...Employers, I now learned were capitalists. They exploited their workers. In the new world that took shape for me at the university, industry was a grim affair of mines and mills, trusts and monopolies...There was menace in the industrial system; there was a need for change...I wanted to change things."[9]

These non-traditional universities provided idealistic voices and ideas for the progressive movement of the twentieth century. However, even the freedom of these non-traditional universities was gradually undermined during the twentieth century as all institutions of higher learning had to seek greater financial endowments to survive. In spite of capitalist influence in higher education, during the 1960s there was a movement inspired by the ideals that still lingered from these progressive institutions. On university campuses, many professors and college students criticized and demonstrated against capitalist power and the injustice they saw in the Vietnam War, civil rights violations in the south, and denials of free speech. But, as we have seen, these reformers did not see that the greatest hazard from capitalism was its weakening of the public philosophy by replacing the value of public service with the value of economic self-interest.

Today, more than ever, corporations and/or government are the main sources of economic support for educational institutions. Professors live under a rule of objectivity in which they are limited as to how freely they can express their own opinions. Scholarship and scientific methods are prized over activism for social reforms. Any passionate or emotional public opinion is looked upon with suspicion as being unscientific. The power elite or corporate control of ideas continues on, and the reforms of the past have failed to stop them. Most of the more liberal, technological corporations are no exception. For them, as for all corporations, the economic "bottom line" determines their final social policies. Liberals may control the social values, the linguistic expressions, and most of the airwaves; but the economic conservatives control national and international politics and finance.

Personal Reflections On Higher Education: In 1990 I went back to school to earn my Masters Degree in Political Science at San Jose State University. I had not been in college for thirty-four years. The classes I took were not much different than those I took in the 1960s. I studied political theory, international relations, and research methods in the social sciences. What was most interesting was reading the books that were most respected for their modern perspective on politics. They used the scientific terminology: "sea changes," "paradigms," and "systemic changes." One book I read was written in such a convoluted manner that what the author said in about a hundred pages could have been said simply and in a straightforward manner in one chapter. These modern political theorists were agonizingly trying to write in scientific language. I thought, "Politics! It can be studied scientifically?" I could not see how politics, involving so much emotion and opinion, could possibly use the scientific method and arrive at any real political understanding.

In science you have to have controlled experiments, factual data, and predictable outcomes. I had to laugh thinking about how to apply these principles to a party convention or even analyzing the procedure of the Senate. In political science you deal with people, power, love, hate, revenge, grief, arrogance, pride, ambition, ideals, compromise, etc. How can you measure and record these emotions and human interaction in a scientific manner? I was told by one of my professors that if I wanted to go on for my Ph.D., I should switch to the University of California campus at Santa Cruz and enter the school of humanities. If I had continued on in political science, I would have had to spend all of my time creating polls and surveys and analyzing data.

I have noticed in life that when we distort reality and try to fit it into a particular box, we lose all common sense. All of us have our favorite ideas of life or our preferred perception of reality. When we try to squeeze everything into one idea, we lose our ability to use our experience and intuition to guide us. By political scientists trying to study politics with strictly scientific methods, they have had to leave out the most important parts of politics in order to make their conclusions fit into a controlled box. Another example of lost common sense is the zero tolerance in schools for guns, drugs, etc. By making such an extreme, overly specified rule, principals and teachers are not able to use common sense. A few years ago children were being expelled for having a squirt gun or an aspirin. If the rule said there would be no dangerous weapons or illegal drugs, authorities could have used some of their own judgment. A box keeps people from thinking.

Elementary and Secondary Education: Traditional verses Progressive:

Education is a very complex subject to tackle. I will only cover those aspects that relate to our study of the loss of the public philosophy. We will need some historical background to set the stage for new understanding. E.D. Hirsch, in his scholarly book, *The Schools We Need*, describes the tension that has always existed in educational circles. "For as long as there has been a historical record, educational theories have wavered in emphasis between two opposed but equally important needs in schooling: rigor and flexibility."[10] American education has always been a combination of these two theories. While its educational system retained some balance between the two, the traditional and the progressive approach, American public education served this country well. Since it has been controlled by the progressive or liberal ideas, it has served America poorly.

Test scores across the nation have fallen. In the industrialized countries of the world, America has been near the bottom in international test scores during the last years of the 1990s. America test scores have been going down since the end of the 1960s. There have been continued efforts to move education back towards more traditional practices, but the liberal educators have succeeded in avoiding these attempts by conservative educators and the majority of American citizens.

Progressive education, which is rooted in Romantic philosophy, has had its greatest influence on American education since the beginning the twentieth century. Romantic philosophy, as discussed earlier, maintains that children have innate knowledge and goodness. Character development and traditions of civility are not very important because if you create an ideal society, children will grow up good. Likewise, if you provide a caring, creative environment in the classroom, the innate knowledge within children will express itself creatively.

Liberal education emphasizes the need to teach the whole child at the expense of teaching the mind. It looks beyond the mind to the emotional and social needs of children and includes a softer, more understanding approach to learning. The Montessori schools are one of the purist examples in the United States of Romantic philosophy applied to education. The children determine much of what they are going to learn, and they influence how they will be taught. There is more freedom and fewer rules than the traditional classrooms. The classrooms of schools and teachers following these models often border on anarchy, especially if their students are poor and children of color. Without the structured and disciplined learning environment, and without the teaching of the public philosophy, American children have become deficient academically and morally.

The traditional approach to education was based on a belief that human nature has a potential for goodness, but that it tends to choose evil over good. The traditional classroom was orderly with clear rules and structure. Traditional teachers depended on repetition, memorization, and drills to impart knowledge to the brain, not draw innate knowledge out of it. Traditionalists in education followed the same rules of learning as the athlete, musician, or dancer. Musicians, athletes, and dancers know that you start with the most basic movement, and through repetition and drills, add more complex moves as each area is conquered. They add layer upon layer of knowledge. The motto is: "practice, practice, practice." Traditional education follows these principles and is based upon a more realistic view of how the brain works and of human nature.

Traditional education was invaded by industrial influences before the Romantic theories began to flourish. Actually, progressive education blossomed in the twentieth century as an answer to the capitalist influences. The goal of industrialists was to use education to gain public support for industrial conglomerates and to train people for jobs in industry. Therefore, education since the late nineteenth century has become more focused on economics and less on political and moral training for citizenship. The Cold War enhanced the more vocational, capitalistic goal of education. In an attempt to answer the Communist menace, economic conservatives united democracy and capitalism. American citizens were made to feel patriotic when they supported the free market economy. Presently, corporate influence has continued to use education to train the minds of Americans to unquestionably accept free market practices and the consumer economy as superior to all other systems.

One thing is certain, education since the Industrial Revolution, and now in the Information Age, has not preserved the public philosophy. Increasingly, since the beginning of progressive education, liberal educators have concluded that children do not need concentrated teaching of civics and ethics. Progressives have concentrated their efforts on creating the ideal environment in which their good character qualities could surface.

On the other hand, industrialists desired to preserve some of the teachings of the traditions of civility. The power elite did not want anarchy. They needed workers with good character qualities to be dedicated to the corporation. However, they purposely weakened the public's understanding of civic responsibility because they wanted to gain control of government. They redefined good character to make citizens more conforming and hardworking to fit industrial needs. Capitalists shifted the goal of education towards preparation for work rather than the imparting of academic knowledge that empowers the mind. They knew that knowledge is power, and they did not want people to have the ability to know when their thoughts were being manipulated.

Traditional and liberal education, although having different methods and immediate goals, have, since the end of the nineties, been used to prepare students for jobs. Increasingly, education has been seen by both approaches to be a means to obtain good occupations. Technical and intellectual training for a job has become more important than learning the historical, philosophical, and political knowledge it takes to be responsible citizens. Furthermore, the traditions of civility have been classified as Christian principles rather than moral principles from natural law; therefore, they have been banned from most schools.

Our educational system is failing to teach children how to think as well as how to behave. C. Wright Mill identified this problem in 1956. He said, "To train someone to operate a lathe or to read and write is pretty much education of skill; to evoke from people an understanding of what they really want out of their lives or to debate with them stoic, Christian and humanist ways of living, is pretty much a clear-cut education of values."[11] Ruling involves thinking about and understanding political and ethical values. Capitalist and liberal values have diminished the ability of Americans to discern which values are most important to maintain popular rule. American citizens would find it difficult to choose the right values when having to choose between the following: cooperation or courage, making money or thinking, watching television or reading, technical skills or political knowledge, self-gratification or self-education, passive acceptance or debate, conformity or questioning, and mediocrity or virtue.

The Next Step For Liberal Education

Education in the United States has gone downhill since the liberal, traditional balance has been eliminated and the liberal, progressive ideas have dominated. When traditional and liberal philosophies were balanced, education remained at a high level. Because liberals have gained a monopoly over education, often using teachers' associations to win school board elections, education has been deteriorating. Their ideas sound so good. Liberal educators are caring and sensitive, and, of course, all parents want their children to feel good about themselves. Instead, what has happened is that children have higher self-esteem while becoming more insensitive to others and more violent. All of the emphasis on self-esteem and using psychological tools has created less educated and more violent students.

It is possible to predict the next step liberal educators will take to improve the education and character of American students. Because their premise is that children are innately good and creative, they will have to find excuses why the present system is not working. Progressive educators have emphasized sensitive, caring treatment towards all students. Teachers have tried to avoid inflicting any wounds on their students' psyches. Therefore, according to the premise, their kind and understanding treatment of children should make students kind and caring human beings. However, instead of an increase in respect and kindness on campuses, there has been an increase of disrespectful behavior, violence, and possession of weapons. In addition, there has been more division among ethnic groups and minorities than ever before. Why have the attitudes and test scores of children continued to deteriorate?

According to the liberals, it cannot be the teachers' permissiveness, liberal, psychological method of teaching, or the social training in the school environment that causes students social and academic failures. Since children are born good, they will be good if treated properly. (The idea that children are born good is a not conscious belief for most educators; it has been subconsciously acquired out of the influence of Romantic philosophy). Some other social circumstances outside of school must be to blame. The other major social experience children have is at home with their parents. Therefore, the conclusion of the liberal establishment in the last few years is that the parents must be failing to give their children the kind of loving treatment and politically correct thinking they are receiving in schools. The solution is not to give parents more opportunities to train their children. Instead, many liberal politicians and educators have decided the government needs to create and fund childcare providers who can guarantee that children will be treated properly and trained to be tolerant of others.

The liberal solution to the problem is to have the government, through licensing and funding of daycare providers, gain more influence over children. Liberals believe that parents are no longer able to raise children correctly. By providing liberally trained childcare providers, the government can assure the most controlled environment in which to raise children. It can best train children for their life's work and provide them with the proper tolerant attitudes towards all multicultural groups.

To accomplish their purposes, a liberally controlled government, through its educational arm, wants to start preparing children for school at an earlier age. They have concluded children are scoring poorly on tests because many parents do not prepare their children properly for school. In addition, once children are in school, liberals think it is better for children to come early and stay for longer hours after school in order to continue the positive influence educators have on them. Since parents are failing to prepare children for life and school, they want the government to take over more of the parental role. It is not only necessary for the "village" to help raise a child, but it is also preferable. The village will do a better job than the parents. Hillary Clinton explains liberal goals in her book, *It Takes A Village*.

Imagine a country in which nearly all children between the ages of three and five attend preschool in sparkling classrooms, with teachers recruited and trained as child care professionals. Imagine a country that conceives of child care as a program to "welcome" children into the larger community and "awaken" their potential for learning...More than 90 percent of French children between ages three and five attend free or inexpensive preschools called ecoles maternernelles. Even before they reach the age of three, many of them are in full-day programs.[12]

The liberal answer is not solving but adding to the moral and academic problems of America's children. Liberal officials and schools are more of the problem than the parents. It is the liberal philosophy that has denied the need for moral and civic training and academically rigorous education. Its faulty premise has resulted in faulty conclusions, and our children and our nation are suffering from the weakness of these Romantic-based, liberal ideas. They undermine many of the values that parents teach at home. Although parents are confused, they are still more suitable to parent than the government and teachers. Once parents understand they have been deceived and manipulated to accept faulty ideas, they will be able to move back towards taking responsibility for the moral training of their children. Moreover, they will be able to insist the schools become academically rather than psychologically focused.

How Is Deception Used In Education?

There is a danger when individuals and groups consciously set out to deceive people through the media. Any kind of planned, social engineering is dangerous to democratic institutions and freedom. Deceptive methods have been very blatant in education. Each time progressive educators experience an attack on a certain method of education, they have changed the name of the method while continuing with the original approach. This happened a few years ago in an effort to hold onto a "whole child" approach to education. For example, conservatives introduced outcome-based education as a solution to low test scores. They spoke of using reference tests to evaluate the learning process. They wanted to focus on results by using test scores.

Liberals immediately adopted the wording for outcome-based methods and then changed the content of what these meant. They created assessments that were more subjective than traditional assessment tests, called performance-based tests. They continued to focus on the process and not the outcome. In this way the teachers had more control over how the students were graded, and who would be retained and who passed on. These subjective tests gave the teachers more control over their ability to protect students who they feared would be emotionally affected by the test results. What is especially upsetting is the conscious use of deception to continue to control the educational system. Liberal educators deceived parents and the public.

Recently, in California, this weak and subjective approach to assessments has been overcome by the California Board of Education who developed new, highly academic content standards and required all districts to use a national reference test to measure the success of each school. The new Democratic Governor, Gray Davis, has supported the restoration of traditional methods and content. It will be difficult, if not impossible, for districts and schools to avoid accountability. One reason for the weakening of liberal control can be explained by complaints by corporations that educators are producing a poorly educated workforce. At least for awhile, it appears liberal, educational propaganda will be eroded. Improving education is a big step towards improving thinking, but we still have a long way to go before we can restore the public philosophy to the educational system.

What All Children Need
From Home And School

The reason children are becoming less civilized is because they have not been taught how to be civilized. Many parents and educators are afraid to deny children what they want—teach them civil behavior—because it may hurt or damage their feelings. Since children are born with a mixture of good and evil tendencies, yielding to their demands encourages the evil tendencies. When children are pampered and spoiled in order to protect them from emotional wounds, they become filled with self-importance. These children will disrespect others and feel that only they are deserving of respect. They will easily fall into exaggerated self-pity when their desires go unmet, or they suffer any injustice. Then the monster, revenge, will rise up out of their self-pity and destroy those they perceive have wronged them. This process shows how the uncivilized, monstrous behavior of Klebold and Harris at Columbine High School evolved.

To keep human nature in check, children must be taught right from wrong. They must have clearly defined moral expectations and appropriate punishments when they break the rules. Children feel good when they do the right thing. They need adults to help them to do what is right by setting clear boundaries. As long as rules are applied fairly, children will not suffer emotional wounds. They will emotionally and spiritually prosper when they have morally educated consciences and have developed the ability to live by their consciences. The focus of educators and parents needs to be on the minds and consciences of children, not only on their psyches.

Chapter 8.

Old and New Morality

As described earlier, various elements slammed together in the 1960s and 1970s to create a new culture and a new morality that is the opposite of the public philosophy. Romantic philosophy, the Hippie Movement, psychology, liberal special interests, the death of John F. Kennedy, and the liberalizing of the Democratic Party crashed together creating a new American worldview. This chapter shall compare the old and new morality. First, we will seek to understand the roots of the old morality in the Judeo-Christian belief system. Secondly, we will study the means by which the natural law defines morality. And thirdly, we will discuss the new morality.

Judeo-Christian Morality

The Judeo-Christian belief system and most monotheistic religions base their moral teachings on divine revelation and instruction from God. Most religions agree on many of the same moral doctrines, and all of them believe that morality is absolute not relative. The Judeo-Christian doctrines are part of the foundation of the moral beliefs that formed the American culture up until the mid-twentieth century. We will review this belief system to discover the religious roots of American morality.

Although Christian teaching cannot be separated from its Jewish influence, in the rest of this chapter, I will refer to American religious beliefs as Christian. These beliefs consist of Puritan, Pilgrim, Quaker, and many revivalists' religious influences. Christian doctrine establishes the fallen nature of man. It states that the first humans were created with a pure and sinless nature, which was in the image and likeness of God. Furthermore, they were created in God's image by having a free will. This free will enabled man (male and female) to choose to obey or disobey God. Without free will, man would have had no choice but to love and obey God. Without free will, man would have been like a robot, not a human. He would not have been able to have any relationship of friendship or love with God. He would have been a mindless and a will-less slave.

According to Christian teaching, the first humans chose to disobey God. As a consequence, they were separated from God and their sinless and good human nature became fallen human nature. When the lower, instinctual nature lacks proper civilizing influence it overwhelms the natural desire for goodness. What I have called in this book, the lower nature, without civilizing influences, is an expression of the fallen nature described by Christian doctrine. Through disobedience, man's human nature became a mixture of good and evil tendencies. These tendencies were like yeast in bread dough. If a child was raised in a loving, caring, orderly, and disciplined environment, the evil tendencies would most likely be kept to a minimum and the good yeast would permeate the child's human nature. If a child were raised in a permissive, abusive, unstructured, neglectful, and/or unpredictable environment, the evil yeast would permeate the child's human nature.

Early Christian doctrine (as well as present Christian doctrine) instructed parents to maintain a firm but loving relationship with their children and told them to teach their children the ways of Jesus. Through godly wisdom and through a love for God and their neighbors, Christian children would grow up with the power to do what was right and resist what was wrong. Of course, the only way to contain the evil in human nature was by providing moral teachings that left no room for excuses. These teachings had to be presented as absolutes, especially to believers in their younger years. Christian moral teachings were presented as objective truths that must be obeyed in order to restrain the evil tendencies in human nature. It was believed that the young, usually more than adults, looked for ways out of being obedient if they were provided with exceptions and excuses. Therefore, children were taught not to steal, lie, cheat, hate, murder, be revengeful, etc. Later, as they matured, some of the more subjective and merciful interpretations of moral principles could be introduced. But it was believed that children needed certainty.

In Christian doctrine, there was the intervention by Jesus on behalf of sinners to save them from sin and offer forgiveness for sin. For the present topic this element is not of concern. What we are analyzing are the various interpretations of the composition of human nature and what kind of moral system is required to create and maintain a civil society. Christian doctrine declares that human nature is a mixture of good and evil tendencies, and that for a society to be civilized, just, courteous, and mannerly it must have a set of transcendent moral absolutes and clearly defined expectations of its citizens. It does not neglect mercy and love, but it would prescribe a balance between justice and mercy that would discourage evil behavior. A good society would insist that irresponsible behavior result in appropriate punishment and consequences.

Natural Law Principles Of Morality

Having reviewed the Christian ideas that lay at the foundation of a civil society, let us look at the kind of societal ideas that were produced by natural law advocates. Natural law theories have their roots in early Greek philosophies. Aristotle especially reflected the method by which natural law theories were developed. Aristotle used the inductive method of reasoning. He observed nature and human nature and drew certain conclusions about the physical, political, and human laws that made things work in a right or wrong manner. In his observation of human nature, Aristotle concluded that man was dual in nature. He observed humans' potential for good or evil. Out of his observation he formulated certain natural laws or laws of nature. The following are some of Aristotle's reflections on nature and man:

> *It follows that the state belongs to the class of objects which exist by nature, and that man is by nature a political animal.*[1]

> *For as man is the best of all animals when he has reached his full development, so he is worst of all when divorced from law and justice. Injustice armed is hardest to deal with; and though man is born with weapons which he can use in the service of practical wisdom and virtue, it is all too easy for him to use them for the opposite purposes. Then man without virtue is the most savage, the most unrighteous, and the worst in regard to sexual license and gluttony.*[2]

> *Thus it becomes clear that both ruler and ruled must have a share in virtue, but that there are differences in virtue in each case, as there are also among those who by nature rule.*[3]

In studying human behavior in the various governments in history and during his lifetime, Aristotle concluded that democracies could never succeed. He drew this conclusion because, by observing human behavior, he found that people in a democracy would have to be good for the democracy to endure. He saw that the natural tendency for democracies was to move towards anarchy. When the citizens ruled, if they were not good, they would begin to vote for those things that would please and benefit them individually instead of voting for those things that promote the common good. It is an example similar to how we see the special interest groups of today promoting their own good over the good of the majority. As each individual demanded his own needs be met, division and dissension would result, which would be followed by anarchy.

There were also positive discoveries in natural laws pointing to the rights of all individuals to possess freedom in certain areas and a kind of equality. Enlightenment philosophers and the Founding Fathers concluded from the natural law that people had inalienable rights. Jefferson referred to a Creator, but he believed human rights were inalienable, based on natural rights derived from natural laws as well. Philosophers during the Age of Reason and Enlightenment period were influenced by the discoveries of science. Initially, all scientific discoveries that we now call physics were considered philosophical discoveries. Therefore, philosophers united physical, moral, and human laws.

Many philosophers reflected on man in the state of nature and what brought mankind to the place of establishing governments. The majority concluded that by nature a compact or contract relationship was established between a ruler or a government and the governed. At first philosophers believed that the people were bound to serve the ruler, but as time passed philosophers concluded that nature revealed the compact between a ruler and his subjects required certain obligations by the ruler to the people. As a result of western philosophers discovering these transcendent truths, the Magna Carta was instituted in England in 1215, and for the first time English civil liberties and rights were established, although in a very limited manner, for the people.

I am explaining this thinking process in order to prepare for the next step of reasoning in relation to our topic about morality. As philosophers considered the nature of things and the laws of nature, they pondered the nature of humans and the laws that ruled them. Enlightenment philosophers and the Puritans cherished the freedom and rights they had gained through Christian ideas and the natural law. In spite of their awareness of human rights, they still observed a need to restrain human behavior by a sense of duty. They were very aware of the tendencies in humans to seek selfish ends. As we have seen, the Founding Fathers were especially concerned about the immoral tendencies in human nature. These tendencies motivated them to create the check and balance system along with putting their hopes in the power of factions to preserve our democratic republic.

Let us look at human nature through the eyes of natural law advocates. By observing human behavior, philosophers concluded that there were certain natural laws that ruled human nature. If people failed to fulfill a responsibility or broke a law and did not suffer any consequences, they found that people did not learn to correct their wrong behavior. They learned that human nature required just punishment to restrict impulsive, criminal, and selfish acts. They noticed that if power were put into the hands of humans without any check on that power by other forces, humans would abuse that power. Therefore, politicians would end up promoting their own welfare instead of the welfare of the people they represented. This to the philosophers was a natural law based upon the observation of the natural behavior of humans when there were no restraints.

They further concluded through the natural law that human behavior was predictable, and it was the same for all humans. All humans required the same laws and codes with consequences to preserve order and justice in a society. Since all humans were the same, sharing the same human nature, and all humans would always be the same; transcendent, absolute moral principles and laws were required to tame the nature of all humans. These moral laws would have to be unchanging and absolute because humans were quick to blame others and excuse themselves for their wrongdoing. If someone at that time had proposed that morality was relative, Enlightenment philosophers and our ancestors would have rejected such an idea as not only wrong but foolish. They would have known that such a definition of morality could only lead to anarchy and moral demise. They would have known that if morality were situational, humans would always find a way to excuse themselves from taking responsibility for their indiscretions. The natural law tended to reveal the same findings as Christian doctrine. Although philosophers did not speak of a fallen nature, they observed something in human nature that required restraint and laws to keep humans doing what was right.

Why Morality Must Be Based On Absolutes

The important question to ask at this time in history is: Are Christian doctrine and natural laws accurate? Is human nature in need of moral absolutes? Must the conscience be tuned to transcendent moral values to assure a civil and good society? Is it necessary to have predictable consequences for wrong behavior to avoid the moral breakdown of a society? Let us observe some recent trends in order to answer these questions.

Campaign money provided for political races is a good example of the power money has to entice the greedy and power-hungry parts of human nature. We have seen many politicians sell out constituents and even our country to receive enough money to stay in power. Human nature cannot be trusted to stay honest when provided with enormous amounts of money and the power it buys. Very few people, even those with the best intentions, can resist the worshipful attitudes, power, and comfort provided by fame, wealth, and position. Situational ethics cannot furnish the clear-cut standards that hold human nature in check at moments of greatest temptations. The wily, excuse-creating, self-deceptive tendencies in human nature will reach for any means to fulfill the impulsive and lustful desires to live at the top.

Our society is rampant with examples of people refusing to take responsibility for their actions. The recent suing of tobacco companies is another area in which individuals today have become irresponsible. Adults are sending terrible messages to children about blaming others for decisions that are each individual's own responsibility. Smokers have known for years that cigarettes cause cancer, but some did not take the steps to stop smoking. Now they or their families are getting rich for failing to take responsibility for their own choices. They are blaming cigarette manufacturers and winning big settlements.

Suing gun manufacturers has a different twist. By suing gun manufacturers, people are saying that the individuals who did the killings or shootings are not completely responsible for their actions. Some of the blame is transferred to gun manufacturers. Consequently, society directs less condemnation upon the perpetrators of violent acts. All of the force of societies' condemnation and shame needs to be directed to those who act violently. It is the judgement of society that helps restrain others who consider murdering in the future. As the outcry against guns continues to increase every time there are massacres or children killing each other, the moral pressure which prevents people from committing these crimes diminishes. Criminals can blame others for their actions, weakening the moral power to hold back their violent tendencies.

Finally, the aftermath of the shootings at Columbine High School provides another example of irresponsible and irrational behavior. There is one last lesson to be learned from that event. Since the tragedy, educators and psychologists have responded by seeking ways to prevent this behavior in the future. Their main emphasis has been to sensitize students in schools to the needs and feelings of outcast students. By pointing to the need for sensitivity, who is being held responsible for the shootings? Are the shooters being blamed or are the students who were insensitive being blamed? Obviously, the students being held responsible are those who teased and mocked the "Trenchcoat Mafia."

What is the message being sent to students? They are being told that if all students behave perfectly towards each other, there will be no violence. Since the shootings, students have been made to feel that the lack of sensitivity, not the evil intent of the shooters, is responsible for mass killings at schools. The evil tendencies in human nature are being ignored, and the burden to change is being placed upon those students who were the victims, not the students who devised evil plans. Consequently, those students who feel like outcasts are being sent a message that they have a valid reason for wanting to hurt or kill other students. In actuality, this message which relieves the killers of responsibility, tells students that Klebold and Harris were justified in taking lives. Not that this is the intention of those in education who are working with students to prevent future violent acts. Yet, it will be the subconscious message picked up by the students. If anything, this message will make outcasts more outraged at abusive treatment and feel more justified in acting out.

In observing the weaknesses in human nature, we should develop ways to deal with anti-social behavior that will prevent its weaknesses. Students should be told that the killers were wrong no matter how badly they were treated. No treatment can ever justify such evil behavior. Students should be told that Klebold and Harris had become sociopaths. They had become so bitter, envious, and hateful that they became monsters without consciences. Students should learn how evil thoughts can be fed by video games, music, and movies and told to avoid those things. They should learn that possessing good character and doing what is right is most praiseworthy and seeking revenge is evil and unacceptable. They should be told to love others and to learn to forgive those who treat them unjustly, just as Ghandi, King, and, of course, Jesus did. Only moral absolutes taught and modeled can keep humans from becoming captives to the darker side of their natures. We owe it to our children to provide them with the power to resist their darker side. We must provide them with the map to follow to become good human beings.

In Conclusion: Americans must look to the past to find the universal tones or standards by which to tune American consciences. Both the Judeo-Christian and natural law heritage of the United States confirms that human nature is not good and never will be good. They both agree that to produce the best from human nature and restrain its evil tendencies, there must be an absolute moral standard to guide behavior. If the majority of Americans agree human nature is a mixture of evil and good tendencies, then they need to realize the present acceptance of situational ethics is undermining moral behavior in America. The evil in human nature is not an insignificant attitude that can be corrected by psychology. It is a dark and powerful force that can murder, maim, and cripple other human beings. We must not take it lightly or think it will disappear because people are told to or manipulated to change their attitudes. Evil can only be contained and controlled by a well-informed conscience, the use of appropriate guilt and shame, a clearly defined moral code, instructions on good manners, and the appropriate reward or punishment for doing what is right or wrong.

The New Morality

The new morality is founded upon a new love: love of self. The old morality was founded on love of God and one's neighbor and/or the Golden Rule (Enlightenment ideal). The public philosophy contained social, political, and moral guidelines. When it dominated the American consciousness, it put conscience and principle before personal desires. When self-love dominates a belief system, it places others, neighbors, and family as less important than oneself. Self-love and self-importance are the doctrine of this new morality, and it has permeated the consciousness of the Baby Boomer generation. Love of God and/or the Golden Rule is a love that takes people out of themselves. Self-love makes people have an exaggerated perspective of their own importance. In the Christian context, believers know that their God and their neighbor comes before themselves. Paul, in his letter to the Philippians, said, "Do nothing out of selfish ambition or vain conceit, but in humility consider others as better than yourself. Each of you should look not only to your own interests, but also to the interests of others."4

I remember feeling passionately about a phrase I once saw in the 1960s on a serigraph by Sister Mary Corita, an artist in the Immaculate Heart of Mary religious community. It said something like, "That's what we have to tell them. We must go and tell them that they are immensely, immensely important." The author of this statement was speaking about telling the common man, especially the poor and disadvantaged, how "immensely, immensely important" they were. At that time, I took this idea to heart and joined many other liberals in making this statement a reality. This idea of importance was poured into the psyche of the generations following the

1960s. Educators emphasized it, books were published encouraging it, and television, music, and movies broadcast the message that everyone was equally important.

It is now time to evaluate the results of this experiment of promoting self-love and self-esteem. We have discovered that treating people with deference and exaggerated importance produces individualistic, self-absorbed, and self-pitying people. We have found that human nature cannot handle too much praise without becoming narcissistic. It is easy to get "high" on oneself. Then, any suffering or injustice becomes intolerable. The value of suffering to enhance the development of good character becomes a foreign, unfathomable idea. People with a sense of over-importance resent anything that stands between them and their happiness, and happiness is defined as the absence of pain and the presence of any desired object. They feel entitled to happiness.

With the doctrine of self-love and self-importance, the followers of the new morality cannot see the value in those moral principles that require sacrifice and saying no to one's desires. They see little value in self-denial and self-sacrifice unless there is personal, immediate self-gratification. In other words, they have become more like animals, controlled by instinct and emotions not reason. Many have lost the capacity to sacrifice for the good of another, even one's own children. Trustworthiness, responsibility, honesty, and respect require self-sacrifice. These ethical values require a person to do what is right even when it takes a long time and gives no assurance of success. To follow these values, a person has to give up the easy path. He has to use noble means to achieve his goals.

Following the liberal moral code can be compared to a person going to dinner at a smorgasbord or buffet. There are multiple ethical values offered on the table, and the participants are able to pick which values they choose to obey at any given time. They can skip the first courses and eat only dessert or eat only the first course. It is up to the participants to apply the rules as they go, basing their decisions on what feels good not what is right. They can obey one ethical value one time and ignore it the next time. Feelings and instincts guide their choices rather than reason and the conscience.

Traditional morality has always been presented as a full course meal. Previously, people were encouraged and taught to eat or obey the values that were placed before them. These transcendent, ethical standards had been proven through time to be the healthiest and most satisfying moral food. If the participants ate or obeyed those moral principles, their consciences did not cause them spiritual indigestion. Their decisions were based upon centuries of spiritual and rational exploration of moral absolutes. By judging these values with reason rather than emotional and instinctual urges, moral people consumed the ethical meals served to them. Therefore, their consciences were highly tuned to ethical standards, and they were able to make moral decisions based upon absolute standards in every situation.

When the new morality rules people's actions, the conscience is completely out of tune. Happiness, not good character, is the only meaningful goal. The conscience is not taught what is truly right and wrong; instead, it is taught that right is what feels good and wrong is what feels bad. As a result, the conscience cannot send out the warnings and feelings of shame and guilt to assure righteous conduct. Many people end up "doing their own thing" and following the lower, instinctual, impulsive part of their nature.

In the new morality, if there is a common standard, it would be that a good person is one who cares about the poor, the disadvantaged, the weak and social injustice. A good person seeks equality for women, people of color, laborers, and the disabled. A person is good who cares about any group who is believed to be under-represented. Moral values have been replaced by political and social values. What were once considered moral norms—love, honesty, faithfulness, responsibility, respect, and trustworthiness (the main course)—are increasingly seen as morally neutral. What were once considered social and political values—tolerance, caring, happiness, freedom, equality (mainly dessert)—are increasingly perceived as the moral norms for goodness.

Many times issues concerning political and social values do include moral principles. Slavery, segregation, child labor, and low wages are moral, political, and social issues. There are others, though, that are morally neutral: the space program, a balanced budget, location of a new plant, and educational methods. Many times an issue or plan can be morally neutral and later become a moral issue. For example, if a corporation downsizes and lays off workers because of hard times, it is a morally neutral, social action. If a corporation downsizes during good times, while at the same time exorbitantly increasing the pay of the CEO and management, it becomes a moral issue.

Therefore, political and social values can take on moral tones, but the judge and standard that makes them moral issues come from a higher moral standard. The social and political areas of morality are a small part of the whole ethical picture of human behavior. Daily life decisions require numerous moral choices. Every day there are decisions that need to be made whether one should lie, be responsible, show respect, be trustworthy, give love, be honest, and on and on. If our moral system mainly consists of social and political values, (i.e., concern for the disadvantaged or weak), the most important and most numerous situations requiring moral choices will have inadequate guidance. The conscience will be a weak tool to influence ethical conduct.

Presently, as a society, we are moving towards the conclusion that people can break moral laws, but if they care about the underprivileged and promote freedom and equality, they are viewed as good and righteous. Whether or not a person obeys the moral laws regulating sexual behavior, stealing, lying, blaspheming, slandering, unfaithfulness, or cheating does not determine that person's goodness. In this new morality, people can be moral by just voting or giving money. They do not even have to get personally involved with a disadvantaged person. Moreover, it has become acceptable for people to disobey moral principles, such as honesty, responsibility, respect, and truthfulness, as long as they disobey these principles while helping those who are victims—a good end justifies immoral means. An immoral person in the old sense of the word can be considered morally good in the new sense of the word.

For example, the defenders of Clinton found it difficult to defend his goodness in the Lewinsky scandal because he had betrayed his wife. Still, his supporters fought to protect him because he was a champion of the poor, women, and people of color. His defenders believed he lied to the American people in order to remain in power, so he could continue his benevolent, political goals. The goodness of his political goals outweighed his indiscretions. His protectors felt the higher good of keeping Clinton in power justified their own choices to lie. Very few of his defenders showed signs of guilt or moral indecisiveness while they were lying on television in front of millions of people. Their consciences were regulated by relative, subjective values.

The subjective, so called moral values of our present society are social and political values, not truly moral ones, but liberals identify these values as moral. In fact, they have been turned into religious doctrines. Liberals have become religious fanatics when it comes to their new morality. That is why being politically correct is such a powerful tool against free speech. Any criticism directed at an underdog or minority group, or directed at a liberal leader by conservatives, any neglect or abuse of the environment (and recently, animals as well), and any criticism of gays produces fervent, moral outcries. The more traditionally, moral individuals in the nation who point out true moral failures are called conspirators and mean-spirited. They are portrayed as bigots, and uncaring enemies of the weak. The public buys these misconceptions because their minds have been conditioned to this new morality.

Personal Reflections On The Moral Standard Of Love

Moral actions in natural law and religious thought receive their direction from the highest law, the law of love. Love demands consistency and justice when it is expressed. Love does not allow a person to be kind and forgiving to one person or group and hate and despise another. Caring for the weak is not the same thing as unconditional love that rules behavior towards all people. Love brings all actions into moral uprightness.

If a person loves the underprivileged, can he regularly lie to help them? When someone loves, can he choose to love some people and reject others? Can he have one standard towards those he loves and another standard towards those he chooses to hate or despise? Can a person be loving and have sex with multiple partners? In religions and earlier philosophies, love is seen as a moral attribute equally directed towards all people. It has always been seen as the one moral principle that contains all others. To love some and hate others is contrary to the true nature of love.

Love sees every person as equally deserving of love. One cannot love and consistently break promises. One cannot love and disrespect another. One cannot love and betray a spouse. One cannot love and slander a person's reputation. One cannot love others while loving oneself more. Love serves humbly, builds up, corrects, speaks the truth, puts others first, overlooks wrongs, is trustworthy, forgives easily, gives freely, and lives righteously. No one can be filled with love and then lie, cheat, steal, deceive, mislead, betray, and murder. In other words, no one can be filled with love and use any means necessary to achieve a desired goal—no matter how worthy that goal appears. Noble causes demand noble means.

Disappointing, Shallow Motives

Remarkably, one of the main reasons true morality has been undermined is the result of the sexual revolution. When drugs and free love came onto the scene in the 1960s and 1970s, it appealed to the lower, animal nature of Americans. The 1970s were ten years of sexual anarchy: singles' clubs, one-night stands, gay bathhouses, sexual excess, and finally, AIDS. The sexual revolution caught fire, and it surged through the whole population.

The desire to follow unrestrained sexual instincts requires that other moral laws and principles be abandoned. A person cannot participate in free love and remain faithful, honest, responsible, respectful, loyal, and trustworthy. A small number of citizens (mostly an elite, artistic, celebrity, intellectual group) has nearly succeeded in causing Americans to throw off what this group perceived were puritanical inhibitions. Robert Stein wrote, "Our Puritanical Patriarchal Heritage has cast a heavy shadow on sexuality and the body. This projection of the shadow onto sexuality has had a profound effect on the American psyche."[5] Stein supported the sexual revolution because he saw sexuality as a "great power. In contrast to our monotheistic Judeo-Christian tradition, paganism honors all the gods. Jung's archetypal perspective has made us aware that the soul is essentially pagan and that many aspects of the soul suffer from neglect when we worship only one god." He goes on to explain the revolution of the 1960s: "…the youth of our nation initiated a great revolution which threatened to overturn the powerful puritanical work and anti-sexual ethics of our American culture."[6] Stein exalts in the return of our citizens to paganism and hedonism.

Many in the entertainment industry, as has always been the case, sought to popularize the sexual practices of many in its ranks. During the 1960s and 1970s, there was an instrument available to seduce the Americans and appeal to their sexual desires. It seems so shallow and irrational to think that much of the moral revolution has been driven and motivated from a desire for sexual freedom. I would not believe this would be such a powerful motive if I had not personally observed its revolutionary surge in the 1960s and followed its progression to the present.

The sexual motive for revolutionary change only appears irrational if it is seen simply as sexual pleasure. Sex is more than physical desires and pleasure. Sex is also a door to receive power. People not only get high on sexual pleasure, but they also get high on sexual power. In an unguarded moment, I heard some women journalists on a television show say they thought Clinton was very sexy, and they would not stop for a moment from having sex with him. It was all the more appalling because they indicated that they personally knew Hillary. Yes, pleasure was on their minds, but more so, it was the feeling of power from having sex with the most powerful man in the world. Sex in the form of lust and power are both addictive. Sex is a powerful force in the lower part of human nature. There is an elite who continues to work to transform the moral code of the whole society in order to fulfil their own desires for sexual freedom; and the media has been used to accomplish their purposes.

In Conclusion: Americans will have to restore and renew the culture handed down from their forefathers. These ancestors had traditions of civility received through centuries of religious and philosophical thought. They knew how to tune the conscience to a well thought out and clearly defined moral standard. In chapter three, the conscience was compared to a guitar. The strings of the conscience were shown to be out of tune when a child is born. As children are taught what is right and wrong, their consciences are tuned to an objective, absolute moral standard just as the strings of a guitar are tuned to universal tones. If relative moral principles are used as the tuner—the standards for moral behavior—then the conscience remains out of tune.

If there were an orchestra in which every instrument was tuned to its own pitch or tone, its music would be dissonant and chaotic. So with the conscience, if everyone has their own standard of right and wrong, moral conduct becomes unpredictable and chaotic. This is the society in which we live today. Many Americans have little conviction about how they should behave, and they are uncertain about what to expect from the behavior of others. Therefore, they have become divided because there is no common standard on which to base trust. Since they have their own relative view of right and wrong, they are not able to act in harmony.

Disharmony and distrust are the product of the new morality. Many new laws, which limit freedom, have been created to protect citizens from each other. For example, overbearing laws are made trying to prevent politicians from keeping information from the public. In California, there is a law called the Brown Act that sets down detailed rules to keep political committees, boards, and commissions from doing things behind closed doors. No more than two members can talk to each other about any impending decisions outside of a public session without violating that act. It makes it nearly impossible for members of boards to build a relationship or reach an understanding with other members. Yet, it is necessary because the members still find ways around or behind the Brown Act to exclude the public from its decision-making process. The new morality invites anarchy, and consequently, it necessitates increasing laws to restore order. Only by increasing laws, control, and regulations can our society remain civilized.

The old morality inspired the best in people and restrained their evil tendencies. Therefore, our Founding Fathers were able to create a democratic republic instead of some form of aristocratic rule. To live in a free country, Americans will have to return to the old, absolute morality and give up the wrongful pleasures they have learned to enjoy. They have to abandon the power that lies and deception give them. They have to abandon the flexibility provided by dishonesty. They have to abandon their freedom from feeling guilt and shame, and their enjoyment of career challenges to the neglect of their children. They have to abandon the love of money, the love of possessions and homes, and generally, the enjoyment of numerous irresponsible habits. Once they choose to find the moral path again, other fears and confusions will fall away and be replaced by a sense of peace and self-respect for doing the right thing.

Chapter 9.

The Failure of Churches to Maintain the Public Philosophy

Puritan And Pilgrim Influence In Creating The Public Philosophy

The Judeo/Christian belief system, more than all other religious systems, has had the strongest influence on the moral values and traditions of civility in the United States. Its history begins with the Pilgrims and Puritans coming to this continent in search of religious freedom. They were not only on a search; they had prophesies telling them to come to this new world. They believed God directed them to America, where they would find a "new Heaven and new Earth." The Puritans believed God sent them to this new world as expressed in the following:

How much more shall Christ who creates all power, call of this 900 league ocean at his pleasure, such instrument as he thinks meet to make of us in this place, from whence you are now to depart, but further that you may not delay the voyage intended, for your full satisfaction know this is the place where the Lord will create a new Heaven, and a new Earth in, new Churches, and a new Commonwealth together,...[1]

When they arrived, both Pilgrims and Puritans entered into a covenant with God. The Pilgrims, in the Mayflower Compact of 1620, made a covenant to serve God and each other by planting a colony in this continent. Their covenant was not only a compact uniting the colonists in love, but it was also a compact to form a civil government. The Pilgrims and Puritans were spiritual but also very practical. The Christian principles by which they led their lives were to be applied to the forming of a "civil body politic." Their end was to plant a colony that would be established for the "glory of God and the advancement of the Christian Faith and honor of our King and country,..."[2]

Christian values were the standard for the manners, norms, and moral conduct which were followed in everyday life and in the governments they formed. They promised to live differently than and more righteously than Christians and non-Christians in Europe. John Winthrop wrote "A Modell Of Christian Charity" on the Arrabella as the Puritans arrived in New England in 1630. In it, he expressed the mutual covenant that the new settlers had with God and each other. They promised "to doe Justly, to love mercy, to walke humbly with our God, for this end, wee must be knitt together in this worke as one man,..."[3] They would make this country a "City on a Hill" that would shine as a beacon, revealing God's goodness. The colonists would reveal God's goodness in their lives and in their institutions through the blessings God bestowed on them, his chosen people. Early colonists saw themselves as similar to the Jews; they were God's chosen people—called out from among those Christians who had taken godly traditions and replaced them with man-made traditions.

As the years passed, when anyone immigrated to this country (no matter what their religion or non-religion), they were immersed in the religious and Enlightenment heritage and morals of our country's first settlers. The public philosophy was integrated into the worldview of every immigrant. Revivals cropped up whenever a new group of immigrants needed to absorb the religious part of the American Dream. In addition, periodic generations had to experience a renewal and revival of moral laws and Judeo/Christian doctrines. There were constant reminders as to the special nature and calling of this country. This nation was created by God for the benefit of the needy masses and for those persecuted for their religious beliefs. Through spiritual revivals and political debate, Americans were constantly reminded of their moral and civic duties, and their consciences were repeatedly tuned to universal moral laws and principles.

Fundamental Christian principles have held sway in America through the first three hundred years of its existence despite materialistic distractions, scientific and philosophical attacks, and the Industrial Revolution. Although theologians, philosophers and scientists kept up a continuous barrage of questioning and disputes among themselves, most grassroots American believers held onto their faith and continued to win converts. New Christian denominations rose up to express Christ's compassion by meeting the spiritual, social and physical needs of each new immigrant group. The questioning and disputes failed to saturate the lives of believers because their local churches had more influence than intellectuals did with their abstract reasoning.

Twentieth Century Influences

The twentieth century has provided increased challenges to Christian churches to retain the Judeo/Christian moral influence in civil government and individual lives. Historically, its value system has been under attack by philosophers and atheists. However, more inroads have been made in the twentieth century because of the far-reaching power of the media. The media does not always attack Christian values directly; it just represents non-Christian lifestyles as more acceptable and normal. Of course, there are times that the attack on Christianity is direct. Earlier I referred to the industrial and Romantic philosophies of the nineteenth century that questioned the existence of absolute moral principles and espoused moral relativism. In the following sections, we will review two other attacks on Christianity.

Humanism

The twentieth century propelled humanist ideas, which had formerly been kept to the extremities, into the center of the American Christian consciousness. The ideas of humanism had been around as long as there were thinkers. However, in the twentieth century, these ideas began to permeate American consciousness through the use of modern communication technology and by the increase in college-educated citizens.

A religious humanism was formulated, using scientific notions from sociology and psychology. It was a religion based on natural, human knowledge that aimed at replacing religions which were based on supernatural knowledge. In Humanism, it is believed that God does not exist, and there are no absolute moral principles. Moreover, through new scientific discoveries and the enlightenment of the scientific spirit, Humanists believe man can achieve the "enlightened fulfillment of human needs."[4] The goal of religion should be to help society meet the challenges of the modern age, not seek to please a transcendent God.

In his book, *Religion and American Society*, Thomas H. O'Connor explains that "In the twentieth century, the movement to de-emphasize the supernatural and denominational aspects of organized religion in favor of a more humanistic and scientific approach greatly intensified." Then, in 1933, some Humanist leaders published "A Humanist Manifesto." They stated that science had replaced old beliefs. Science had shown that the world is "self-existing" and "not created," and man's religion has its source in the natural process of social development. Consequently, the world needs "religious humanism" to replace old ideas which are now out-of-date.[5] Since this new religion reflects modern social changes and scientific knowledge, it is more suitable to enlighten and guide modern man. The goal of Humanism is to help create better societies. Many modern Americans have come to accept the tenets of this new religion without necessarily claiming membership in its ranks. They have come to doubt the existence of a supernatural world, and they have put more confidence in man's power to solve his own problems and guide his own life.

"God is Dead": The "God is Dead" movement became a public discussion in the mid-sixties. Its thesis was that God was dead because he was no longer relevant or necessary in modern society. Western culture was so estranged from its early cultural roots that the idea of a transcendent God was outmoded and impractical. "There was no single or precise definition of this movement. Rather, it covered a very broad spectrum of different ideas and opinions which centered around the belief that the existence of God was no longer relevant to the modern world, and that the individual would have to reconstruct his or her moral view and ethical values on that basis."[6] These ideas were published and discussed on radio and television, and they had a great influence on the public.

The public debate about God being dead was the culmination of centuries of questions initiated by scientific discoveries. During the sixties, through the use of the media, Judeo/Christian thought lost out to liberal and capitalist ideas. The media was used to create phenomena unknown before in American history. The industrial and liberal ideas and Judeo/Christian beliefs were no longer able to co-exist harmoniously in the American consciousness. Presently, the majority of Americans may claim to believe in God or to be Christians, but many are not believers in the traditional sense. They do not connect the moral teachings of Christ to their daily lives or to their duties as citizens. Many of the liberal left who profess to believe in a transcendent God or profess to remain Christians, measure the righteousness of their own and others' behavior by the principle of helping those in need. As discussed earlier, they do not hold themselves accountable to all moral laws and principles but only to the ones they choose.

Are Liberal Christian
Churches An Oxymoron?

Most of the older Protestant denominations in America have been influenced or transformed by liberal dogma. The liberal approach and the Christian approach to life are in disagreement at their premises about human nature—liberalism being rooted in the Romantic belief that human nature is good, and Christianity being rooted in the belief that human nature is a mixture of good and evil. When liberal ideas rule, they cause moral excesses that cannot be made compatible with Christian doctrine. It is impossible to be a Christian and a liberal in the true, philosophical sense of the word liberal. There are liberal Christians just as there are conservative Christians who are not aware of the conflicts between their religious and political philosophies. Many liberals who are Christians have to hold two opposing beliefs in their consciousness. As Christians, they have to believe in the existence of absolute, transcendent moral laws; and as liberals, they have to ignore the application of these laws to some behaviors. Liberal Christians and liberal Christian churches are unclear about right and wrong. They do not judge their members for breaking all moral principles. Because they do not want to make their members feel guilty or ashamed, liberal pastors cannot help their members overcome all of their transgressions. In their desire to show acceptance, they fail to lead their members to a relationship with God that is based upon biblical principles.

Liberal Christian pastors accept the liberal notion that the goodness of a person is judged by that person's concern and treatment of the needy in society. Moral laws about lying or illicit sex are not included in their doctrines concerning sinful behavior. For example, Clinton could be embraced by his church without repenting to the American people for lying and deceiving them. He never admitted to the American people that he lied to them about his affair with Lewinsky. He never said he was sorry for lying to them. He admitted to and asked forgiveness from his wife and daughter. There was enough moral sense left from past tradition to expect him to ask forgiveness from his wife and daughter. Even then, it appeared he never saw the complete picture of how he betrayed his wife since he never thought he committed adultery. Because he cared about the disadvantaged in society, it seemed his pastor did not lead him to look at all of his transgressions. Somehow, the pastor's liberal values allowed him to ignore some of the President's moral failures. Since Clinton had compassionate, political ideals and showed love to the dispossessed, he did not need to face all of his transgressions. Tragically, some liberals seem to forget that a man's love should begin with his wife.

These ideas may seem foreign to some of my readers. Let me explain the responsibility of a pastor to someone in his congregation who has sinned, and the responsibility of a Christian who has committed sin. The role of pastors is to help their members know, love, and serve Jesus. They teach the moral principles set down by God and guide their members to successfully obey those principles. They show believers how to obey God from a motive of love. Pastors should not preach a set of laws but rather preach how to follow the law of love. If a person loves God and his neighbor, he will automatically do those things that are loving. He will not need a set of laws to make him do the right thing.

It is the role of a minister to guide his congregation to understand spiritual principles and to follow those principles. If a member of his church falls into sin, it is the pastor's responsibility to lead him through the steps to restore his relationship with God. If a minister allows one of his members to remain in sin without telling him the truth, God holds him accountable for that person's sin. All sin is very important to God because it separates His children from Him. He holds people accountable for their choices because He is not asking them to do anything that he will not give them the power to do. God, through Jesus, provides believers with the power over sin. If a pastor fails to warn and help a member of his congregation overcome immoral behavior, he is doing him a great injustice. By leaving him ignorant, he could be leaving him vulnerable to be eternally separated from God.

It is the responsibility of the person in a transgression to not only look at his objective sin but also at the sin in his heart. The Bible says the "heart is deceitful above all things and desperately wicked."[7] For a Christian to restore his relationship with God and anyone he has sinned against, he must ask forgiveness for his objective sin and his heart sin. By seeing and repenting for his sin, a person is able to receive from God freedom and cleansing from that sin. This is the process Clinton needed to go through. Then we would have known if he had successfully achieved restoration by how he responded to us and his wife. His heart change would be reflected in his actions. If he said he did something wrong (rather than something inappropriate), and if he said he was sorry for deceiving us (the public), then we would know he had made himself right with God. If he did not say those things, then we know that he was not honest with himself or us. If his pastor did not hold him accountable to be truthful about what he had done and allowed him to speak half-truths, then that pastor has done him a great spiritual disservice. It is in situations like these that liberal Christian churches and pastors can do great harm to their members, especially if God does exist and does have expectations of those who call themselves Christians and ministers.

Christianity Fails To
Restore The Public Philosophy

The ethical teachings of Christianity are no longer accepted as the moral guidelines for American citizens or public servants. Since the "God is Dead" controversy, it is has become apparent that many American citizens do not see the relevance of God in their lives. This is especially true of the baby boomers and those who came after them. The scandals involving television evangelists in the 1980s added to the seeming irrelevance of

Christianity. Many of those who were seeking answers through Christian teaching became disillusioned by the sinfulness and greed of those evangelists. It appeared to seekers that being a Christian placed no more ethical responsibility upon a believer than a non-believer. By the end of the eighties, the liberal and capitalist philosophy had moved past the 50% mark in replacing Christian influence.

Although Christianity has been under attack for many years, these outside attacks are not the only cause for failing authority. There are practices within Christian churches that also make them less relevant and powerful. These internal defects have as much, if not more, effect than the outside attacks.

The Religious Right And Conservatives

There have been two groups of Christians in traditional churches during the last twenty years. The first group of Christians we will consider has educated themselves about the liberal agenda and their goals. They have been extremely alarmed and used various strategies to block liberal causes. They have demonstrated at abortion clinics, supported and promoted conservative candidates for local and federal elections, organized grassroots lobbying of legislators to stop the passage of liberal legislation, and used Christian television to alert and educate Christians.

This group of activist Christians, the Religious Right, is a small minority of the total number of traditional Christians. They have made heroic and often successful efforts to stop or slow down the liberal agenda. A very small number in that group are violent extremists. They have given the Religious Right a bad name. One of the major weakness of the Religious Right is the appearance of their being alarmists and irrational. It is not that they have no reason for alarm. The problem is that their emotional warnings cause most Americans to perceive them as fanatics. It is as if these Christian activists see a house on fire (i.e., American morality and culture) and bang on the door to warn those inside the house about the fire. Those inside, American citizens, come to the door and cannot see or smell the fire. It is because the fire is still invisible to them. These Christian activists need to find a way to reveal the fire, to give sight to the blind. They have to find an approach that first educates Americans before it warns them.

The Religious Right needs to have an understanding of the bigger picture. They need to show the faulty thinking in the romantic/liberal ideas. These ideas in their pure, undiminished form cannot work. Human nature is not good and to treat people as if they will do the right thing without possessing morally educated consciences is naïve and simple-minded. Americans no longer consciously believe that human nature is good, but public policies are still formed based upon this belief. Christians in the political arena need to educate citizens in local school districts and in other political forums about those flawed ideas and policies. The public has common sense. They will understand that a faulty premise leads to faulty, unworkable conclusions. The Religious Right, must do more to show the faulty logic of liberal thinking. If they are informed about liberals' unrealistic ideas and their conscious use of the media to brainwash them, the majority will begin to question liberal ideas. This information must be given in a logical, reasonable and non-emotional fashion.

Even more important is the need for the Religious Right to separate themselves from economic conservatism. As mentioned earlier, there are two conservative philosophies. The economic, conservative philosophy has been developed by a power, or corporate, elite. It is no more supportive of the traditions of civility than the liberals. Their ideas are based on self-interest. Out of a motive of self-interest, the capitalist elite supports the practice of those ethical principles that create the best conditions for them to make a profit. For example, many corporations are teaching their employees ethics because committed, energetic, loyal, and honest employees provide companies with the most possibility for higher profits. On the other hand, you will not hear them promote the public philosophy for politicians. If that happened, they could not buy the influence they needed to continue their never-ending obsession to make more money and reach new markets.

The Religious Right needs to make a distinction between economic conservatism and the brand of conservatism they should support. When they hold too closely to the free market, lower taxes, and corporate will; they consequently support the "Establishment" or "power elite" rather than supporting Christian principles. They need to define and demonstrate civil conservatism. In civil conservatism the traditions of civility apply to all situations, personal or public. Fairness, justice, love, honesty, faithfulness, respect, and responsibility are only a few of the principles that should be applied to a relationship with one's neighbors and to local, state, and national issues.

In addition, once devoting themselves to the public application of civil conservatism, the Religious Right and conservative politicians have to hold themselves to the highest standard. They cannot invest so much emotion in their personal causes that they justify using unethical means to establish their ends. They cannot play any "dirty tricks." They cannot lie about an opponent, and they cannot send some extremist out to lie about an opponent. They have to show that they support justice for all people, even for those who would limit corporate power, favor abortion, or disagree with their beliefs.

Civil conservatism supports limiting the power of private corporations and insists they have a duty to their communities and the nation. The Religious Right and Conservative Republicans must hold all corporations, whether national or international, to their responsibility to promote the common good wherever they build new plants. Conservatives must become civil conservatives and acknowledge that traditions of civility apply to every area of life: political, economic, social, and personal. They cannot apply moral traditions to all areas except the economic or political ones.

Inactive Traditional Christians

The other group of traditional Christians, the politically inactive Christians, has a different problem. They have done the opposite of the activists; they have pulled within themselves and their Christian communities. They try to send their children to Christian schools or do home studies, socialize mainly with other Christians, and do not want to know how badly the country is doing. They fail to be models of the traditions of civility for the secular world. They are fearful and feel powerless. Erich Fromm's book, *Escape from Freedom*, gave an excellent description of what happens when the responsibilities of democracy or freedom become too great. He describes the fears of a free people, and his book was "devoted mainly to freedom as a burden and danger."[8] When burdened by freedom (and feeling overwhelmed with the task of ruling), citizens turn over their responsibilities to someone else. These actions open the door to a takeover by an oligarchy, as is happening in the United States.

Christian churches, whose members believe in the salvation message and uphold the standards of the Bible, have another weakness. Because they and their pastors separate themselves from the secular world, they cannot discern the secular ideas that weaken the Christian message. Many members of Christian churches have been strongly influenced by the liberal culture without knowing it. They have been influenced by the liberal beliefs that self-love is a prerequisite to loving one's neighbor, that it is wrong to speak truth that hurts a person's feelings, that guilt and shame are detrimental to healthy self-esteem,, and that wrong behavior is a mistake and not a sin.

The self-centered and selfish attitude of the world is also prevalent in churches. Many pastors in recent years have "burned-out" because their members demand to be served more than they are willing to serve. The needs in a church are so great that pastors depend on volunteers to take on many of the day-to-day responsibilities. Sunday school teachers, Bible-study leaders, group leaders, choir members, ushers, etc. are all volunteers.

Many churches are suffering from their members refusing to serve and to hear any correction about their selfishness. Pastors will have to reach the hearts of their people and bring changes to their hearts if Christians are going to be an example to a self-centered secular culture. The Christian heritage of the traditions of civility will only be effective when modern, liberal influence in churches are exposed and expelled.

THE FAILURE OF PASTORS TO LEAD

Some of the fear and ignorance of Christians is caused by the lack of direction and information given by church pastors. In the past, Christian churches were frontrunners in pointing out error and sin. During the Revolutionary War, the Abolitionist Movement, and labor disputes in the early twentieth century, clergymen were visible and prominent as leaders and spokesmen in these movements. The most recent social action by ministers was the Civil Rights Movement with the foremost leader being the Reverend Martin Luther King, Jr. Religious leaders were instrumental in moving all social movements to successful completion.

In previous times, clergymen preached from the pulpit against injustice and condemned sins in leaders. Now, there is almost no comment on any political events or decisions. We go into wars and out of wars, and there is no questioning or moral response made by the majority of pastors. Newspapers and television newscasts do not quote criticisms by clergymen on the many issues that have faced this nation in the last thirty years. During the Lewinsky scandal, a few traditional ministers came on television to argue with liberal ministers, such as Jesse Jackson. But there was not a spontaneous eruption of religious feelings by ministers nationally. The Reverend Billy Graham expressed an unclear spiritual message, being overly concerned about condemning the sin and not the sinner. The fear of judging others and injuring a person's psyche has infiltrated into the churches.

One might ask what a pastor could say that his congregation did not already know. They knew that Clinton was immoral and committed adultery. They knew he was wrong to lie to his wife and the country. What else might a minister or priest say? The pastor could define the ethical problems in dating relationships and potential temptations for adultery of married couples. I know a number of single people who say they are Christians and who attend church regularly but who have sexual relations whenever they enter a new relationship. Since modern culture has made free sexual behavior appear the norm, it is hard for many Christians to resist these temptations. It needs to be talked about openly. Ministers need to use some publicized situations to refresh Christian consciences. Where else can people receive practical, moral teachings but in churches?

More importantly, pastors need to express the mind and heart of God on all moral questions that come before the public. It is their duty to clarify multiple wrong-minded opinions about morality. For example, the Columbine massacre on April 20, 1999 was the worst massacre at schools to date; and it followed right on the heels of the Clinton scandal. That massacre and the seven other killings at schools could be interpreted by pastors as God's wake up call for this nation. Pastors could teach their congregations that heinous crimes are the result of our judicial system's failure to judge and condemn lawbreakers. Their members could be reminded of the traditions of civility that maintain a civilized society. They, too, need to be reminded to behave in a civil manner at all times.

In the case of Clinton, the Senate failed to hold him accountable to the law. A pastor could draw a relationship between the President's actions, which were above the law, and the increase in lawlessness and violence that has proceeded his exposure and vindication. As we have seen, there are universal, moral laws similar to universal physical laws that, when broken, lead to predetermined, absolutely predictable consequences. For example, we know that apples do not fall off a tree and go up; they fall down off a tree to the ground and become bruised. So also, if the chief executive of our country (who is responsible to enforce the laws of the nation) is deemed above the law, then the estimation of the rule of law falls in the eyes of our citizens. Those who are already unstable and lawless are morally bruised by the example and lose all sense of boundaries. Some are taken over with obsessions and confusion, leading to violence; others are taken over by evil, leading to hideous crimes.

Clergymen could use the Clinton scandal, the Columbine tragedy, or other public traumas or immoral acts as an opportunity to teach certain godly principles. They could explain how moral laws and principles work. They could reeducate their congregations in the principles of the public philosophy to make them not only better Christians but better citizens. Christians spend too much time trying to please God by making themselves more perfect and sin-free rather than making themselves into a better public or community member. (I know this from personal experience.)

In America, with a republican form of government, Christians have a duty to apply the traditions of civility they have learned in their churches to their communities and nation. They may be Christians first, but God chose this nation for a mission, and they are part of that mission. They need to restore this nation to being the "City on a Hill." Pastors will have to become less concerned with the growth of their churches and the cleansing of their people and decide to take their light into the world where it belongs. Ultimately, the spiritual growth of their members will only come through unselfish acts of love directed towards those less lovely.

Why Pastors Are Not Leading:

Where is the spiritual and moral leadership for this time? Why are pastors remaining passive and silent? First, for a minister to speak out against sin in the government or sin in those governing, he would have to show the emotion of anger and outrage. Presently, emotional expression, even when justified and appropriate, is frowned upon as irrational and unhealthy. The suppression of righteous emotion is also caused by the liberal anathema towards judging others. Liberals insist there are no objective, moral principles by which to judge a person's behavior. The public philosophy, which established and maintained the American civil society since its founding, can use history to prove otherwise.

Second, a reason pastors fail to speak out against sin and injustice is because churches are under non-profit laws. Just as colleges are controlled by contributions, and schools are influenced by federal programs, so also there are pressures on churches to avoid certain controversies in order to avoid the loss of non-profit status. Although there is room for moral judgments on issues and politicians, there is still the fear of crossing the legal line. If a pastor criticized an elected official, the criticism could linger during the politician's next election. The church members would have already heard certain judgments on that politician's past actions. Has the pastor broken the law? Possibly, yes. How can the minister now revert to a neutral stance for the coming election? The law appears weak, but its ramifications are broad.

In conclusion, we see that the religious institutions of our society, just as the educational and family institutions, are wrapped in the interlocking liberal and capitalist laws that rule our nation. These three institutions are the last to be swallowed up by the existing oligarchy (rule of a few). The educational system was the first to be taken over by undemocratic philosophies. It no longer imparts to students the lessons required to maintain a republican form of government. Public education is no longer about passing on the historical and philosophical knowledge that makes children think and reason. It does not give knowledge of the traditions of civility and the clear purpose of community service that formed the goals and character of earlier Americans.

Unfortunately, progress has been made in undermining parents and families. Parents are being pushed and enticed into the workplace while their children are being taken away from them by liberal programs turning schools into health, social, and community centers. Liberal educators and other liberals plan to make schools the center of children's lives, providing occupational preparation, family substitutes, and a culture of self-love. As mentioned earlier, parents are being undermined by both liberals and conservatives. Liberals want to raise children in place of the parents, and conservatives are driving children into the arms of liberals by supporting the excesses of the free enterprise system. "Those on the right simply do not understand that government must play a pivotal role if we are to develop the social supports we need to counter the family-destroying and parent-displacing properties of the market. Bolstering the earning power of child-raising adults is just one of the ways in which government must intervene if moms and dads are to be effective and wholehearted parents."[9]

With public education already swallowed up in undemocratic philosophies and financially pressured parents releasing their children into the care of others at an increasingly early age, only the churches remain as the preservers of the traditions of civility; and they are under siege. Those liberals who have entered into the strongest attack on the church are gay special interest groups. They play on the emotions of the public and make people feel they are right about their demands, even when their demands are irrational and illogical. As mentioned earlier, they are seeking to divide Christians by forcing their acceptance in churches. Gays and other liberals are gaining support from lawmakers and the executive branch of the federal government.

Persecution of Christians is on the increase, and persecution of all traditional religions will surely follow. Pastors need to demonstrate courage and leadership. This is no time to accept the liberal idea that a leader is a facilitator. Pastors and priests will not be able to turn around this attack unless they instruct their congregations, take them out of their quiet surroundings, and lead them into contributing in their communities. Christians can only be salt in the world by being in the institutions and organizations of the secular world. Serving in one's community should be a natural activity. Christians should join organizations, volunteer to do charitable work, run for office, mingle with

Non-Christians with the intention of helping, not converting. The prophets in the Old Testament repeatedly cried out for Zion to awaken; they sounded the alarm. The Church needs to take its role in the restoration of the public philosophy and reestablish the religious morality that has historically been a part of the American character.

Chapter 10.

What It Will Take to Restore American Culture

To restore the public philosophy to our nation, Americans need to seek in our heritage the truths that laid its foundation. We must find the God-Formed and self-evident truths that all people are created for a purpose, and that purpose is to contribute to and serve one's family, one's neighbors, one's community, and one's nation. We are endowed with duties to protect individual rights and promote the common good. We are called to cultivate the qualities and habits of good character, giving ourselves over to forming an upright conscience and living by the highest moral principles of love, courage, and duty. We must take up the standard raised by John F. Kennedy and finally answer his summons to ask how we can serve our country and its citizens rather than ask how we can be served. That is the Kennedy legacy, and it is time to fulfill it.

A Review Of The Thesis Of This Book

For most people who have been alive since before the 1940s, there is no question that there has been a revolution in American culture, what Frances Fukuyama calls the, "Great Disruption," in his book by that name. Before moving on to prescribe ways to reverse the present revolution in American culture, we will review the conclusions that have been reached in defining this problem. We have seen that there have been three philosophies fighting for preeminence in the American consciousness. First, the foundational philosophy in America's beginning was the Judeo-Christian and Enlightenment mixture believed and practiced by the first colonists and later, with an Enlightenment emphasis, by the Founding Fathers. In this book, this mixture has been called the public philosophy or the traditions of civility.

Our forefathers believed there was a God who had established this world and its moral precepts, which could be known through divine revelation and/or natural laws. They saw human nature as a mixture of good and evil tendencies, so a check and balance system—a republican form of democratic government—was created through the Constitution to assure rule by the people. In addition, they believed that customs and moral norms were a necessary part of a successful republican government, and religion was necessary to maintain those customs and moral norms. They agreed with Aristotle that in a democracy the people must be good. One of the founders' greatest fears was that the people would cease to be good, and therefore, lose their ability to rule.

The second philosophy or activity of prominence that was present from the first colonists onward was the mercantile or capitalist ideas. It developed into the economic conservative viewpoint. The early colonists were pleased with their opportunity to improve their material state and own property, but it was not their initial motive for coming to the New World. During the time of the Founding Fathers, there was a more mercantile spirit. A wealthy aristocracy had developed and Alexander Hamilton represented that interest when he proposed a national bank. As time went on, the desire for material improvement became a stronger pull for Americans. Alexis de Toqueville noted that in the 1840s, "One sees them, however, seeking with almost equal eagerness material wealth and moral satisfaction: heaven in the world beyond, and well-being and liberty in this one."[1]

Still, during the period of the writing of the Constitution up until the Industrial Revolution, beginning in the latter part of the nineteenth century, the public philosophy remained the most influential philosophy. The principles of natural law were seen by many as the more convincing argument for the defense of freedom and equality than was the divine compact of our Puritan ancestors, but the public philosophy remained in force.

In the late nineteenth century the industrial philosophies began to be clarified and advertised. They promoted, as they still do today, the free-market economy. Capitalists claimed that fewer government regulations promoted a better economy and prosperity for the largest number. The idea of "trickle down" economics was not named in the nineteenth century, but it was practiced. Science was used to support capitalist ideas; these pseudo-philosophical ideas were called laissez faire and survival of the fittest (Darwinism). The greatest damage this philosophy did to the traditions of civility was to replace the guiding principle of the public philosophy—unselfish, duty-bound dedication to family, neighbor and community—with the idea of "enlightened self-interest." The idealizing of the faulty idea that everyone benefits by everyone following their own self-interest gradually helped undermine the public philosophy. Moreover, when the idea of moral relativism was added to the ideas of self-interest, it added another blow to the traditions of civility.

Another occurrence, which was equally harmful to the public philosophy, was the identification of the public philosophy with economic conservatism and the modern Republican Party. Economic conservatives supported some of the ideas of the public philosophy and ignored others. Their goal was to remove from American consciousness the knowledge of the duties of property owners and corporations to the public. They wanted workers to accept their duties to business, but many businessmen did not want to honor their duties to their workers or society. Of course, if they had accepted the traditional responsibilities of civil conservatism, they would have been responsible and just to laborers. Since they followed economic conservatism, they ignored public well being, and consequently, forced liberal or Romantic ideas into the forefront to protect and promote the rights of workers. If the principles of the public philosophy had been applied to business, this liberal movement would not have been needed.

As we have seen, these Romantic ideas had a faulty premise about the goodness of human nature. It led to the corruption of the moral values, customs, norms, and traditions of civility that are necessary for the preservation of popular rule in this country.

The third philosophy vying for attention in America's history was the Romantic philosophy. Romantic philosophy became the expression of modern liberalism. It held the weakest position at the time of the Founding Fathers. Early liberals, like Thomas Jefferson and the other founders, thought Rousseau's ideas about the state of nature were faulty. Jefferson drew upon Enlightenment or natural law ideas for his statement in the Declaration of Independence more than Romantic ideas. In contrast, the French Revolution was inspired by Romantic philosophy.

Liberalism has grown in power since the advent of the Information Age. Liberals learned to compete with capitalists in the media. They became masterful in their ability to promote their ideas with the same deceptive means as capitalists. Their premise about the goodness of human nature led to the idealizing of man-in-the-state-of-nature. They were critical of western civilization because they believed that man was most creative and reached his fullest potential when he was free from civilizing influences. They believed that humans could be trusted to do what was right by nature, and seeking self-love and self-fulfillment would help them be their best. Authority and leadership was seen as suspect and demoralizing rather than instruments of order. Finally, and most harmful, liberals mistakenly identified the norms and traditions of civility (formulated from the best ideas of western civilization) with economic conservatism and therefore rejected the civilizing ideals and moral absolutes of the public philosophy.

At this time, the corporate capitalists and modern liberals rule our country. The public has been manipulated by both of these groups to obtain support for their various agendas. Neither party, the Republicans or the Democrats, has the answers on how to restore civility to our society or self-rule back to the people. Most politicians cling to their power and have lost sight of their purpose to promote the common good. The Republicans think that the free-market and less government create the best society for Americans. The Democrats are rethinking their philosophy. They are trying to adjust to the global economy while preserving the idea that government should use its power to advance the rights and welfare of the people.

The Information Age has introduced new elements into the national and international scene that are causing confusion on many levels. As we have seen, the power of the media in the Information Age has been used to disrupt the traditional values that hold American society together. The minds of Americans are very vulnerable to media advertising, especially when it is used as a political tool. A sound bite or a falsehood is repeated innumerable times until it becomes a truth to the listener. Most Americans have lost the ability to discern between truth and lies and facts and opinions. They have become what Mills calls, "the masses" instead of the public.

In search of answers to recent violence and antisocial behavior, the moderate Republicans and Democrats increasingly seek practical, physical answers to these disorders. They are unable to look beyond immediate solutions. They are not able to see the condition of the soul and con-science of Americans. As long as the Republican and Democratic Parties continue to accept the same doctrinal guidelines they have followed in the past, the more destructive and ineffective their policies will become.

The faulty premises of economic conservatism and liberalism will increasingly cause social turmoil. If neither party provides leadership in restoring the public philosophy, a new party will have to lead the country back to it. The reintroduction of traditional, moral principles to guide professional, business, political, and personal conduct is the only means to halt the disintegration of American culture caused by capitalist and liberal philosophies. America is being propelled into the future without a map or directions to guide it. It has to find guidance for the journey. According to the philosopher, Machiavelli, a nation must look back to its beginnings, when it was young and innocent, in order to reform the future. Americans can be assured they cannot go wrong by looking back to the public philosophy. This philosophy has never been wrong; it has only been ignored.

Why Restore The Public Philosophy?

Niccolo di Bernardo Machiavelli was a philosopher in the fifteenth and sixteenth centuries. Most people know him from his work, The Prince. Philosophers at that time depended upon the financial and political support of those in power. At the time he wrote, The Prince, Machiavelli was out of the graces of the prince, Cesare Borgia. In order to win the prince's favor, Machiavelli wrote a "handbook for tyrants" in which he advocated the "end justifies the means." Although this particular idea has inspired corrupt leaders since it was expressed, it is not the only idea of Machiavelli worth noting.

In some of his other, more objective and idealistic work, he made an observation that is helpful for our search in how to restore the public philosophy to our nation. It seems only appropriate to use the philosopher who helped demolish the principles of civility and civil government to now aid in the reestablishment of these principles. In The Discourses, Machiavelli outlines how a nation can be renewed after it has been corrupted.

The means of renewing them is to bring them back to beginnings, for all the origins of religious groups, republics, and kingdoms contain within themselves some goodness by means of which they have gained their initial reputation and their first growth. Since, in the course of time, this goodness becomes corrupted, if nothing intervenes that may bring it up to the proper mark, that body is, of necessity, killed by such corruption...This return to beginnings, in the case of republics, is accomplished either by an external event or as a result of internal foresight.[2]

If there are those who think this renewal can be legislated, Machiavelli goes on to explain:

> *...for neither laws nor institutions are to be found which suffice to check a universal state of corruption. For just as good customs require laws in order to be maintained, so laws require good customs in order for them to be observed. Beside this, institutions and laws established in a republic at the time of its foundation, when men were good, are no longer acceptable when men have become evil.*[3]

The answer to preventing our nation from running out of control socially and politically is to return to our beginnings and find the common purpose and common philosophy that brought the United States of America into existence. We have to find our common purpose, our common philosophy, and what was originally considered our common good.

There are two historical groups that formulated our American public philosophy, the Pilgrims/Puritans and the Founding Fathers. Let us review both of their traditions to reevaluate the initial vision and belief system to which Americans need to return.

The Pilgrims and Puritans

The Pilgrims/Puritans believed that God had sent them to a new world with a special calling. They had no doubt as to God's intentions for this new world. Edward Johnson, a historian of the first settlement planted in 1630, often eloquently expressed the sense of calling the Puritans had. He describes "...the immovable Resolutions that Christ continued in these men. . " Those leaving for the new land passionately declared, "I am now pressed for the Service of our Lord Christ to rebuild the most glorious Edifice of Mount Sion in a Wilderness, and as John the Baptist, I must cry prepare ye the way of the Lord,..."[4] Every obstacle, persecution and hardship faced by the Pilgrims was interpreted by

Johnson as the Lord's way of perfecting his spiritual soldiers, "…the Lord Christ intending to make his New England Soldiers the very wonder of this Age, brought them into greater straits, that this Wonder working Providence might the more appear in their deliverance,…"[5]

The fullest expression of the Puritans' purpose in coming to this new land was written by John Winthrop, a leader in the Massachusetts colony. He wrote a covenant of intention to which all of the colonists committed themselves:

> *Thus stands the cause between God and us, we are entered into Covenant with him for this work, we have taken out a Commission, the Lord has given us leave to draw our own articles…but if we shall neglect the observation of these Articles…The Lord will surely break out in wrath against us…*

> *Now the only way to avoid this shipwreck and to provide for our posterity is to follow the Council of Micah, to do Justly, to love mercy, to walk humbly with our God, for this end we must be knit together in this work as one man, we must entertain each other in brotherly affection,…we must delight in each other, make others conditions our own, rejoice together, mourn together, labor, and suffer together, always having before our eyes our Commission and Community in the work, our Community as members of the same body,…The Lord will be our God and delight to dwell among us,…*[6]

John Winthrop went on to declare that if the Puritans followed all of God's precepts and obeyed his commission, God would give them great blessings and wisdom. If they were obedient, the God of Israel would make the New England plantation a praise and glory for all to see. Then, other settlers who would come to America would ask the Lord to make their settlements like the Massachusetts colony. He goes on to proclaim:

*...For we must Consider that we shall be as City upon a Hill, the eyes
of all people are upon us; so that if we shall deal falsely with our god in
this work we have undertaken and so cause him to withdraw his present
help from us, we shall be made a story and by-word through the
world,... Beloved there is now set before us life, and good, death and evil
in that we are Commanded this day to love the lord our God, and to
love one another...that we may live and be multiplied, and that the
Lord our God may bless us in the land whether we go to possess it.*[7]

The first Christian settlers lived by principle. They were intent on
planting a new, godly society the likes of which had never been seen in the
history of the world. Their goal was to form a government, community,
and church that would bring glory and praise to God. The articles by
which they lived were clearly defined by the principles of love. They had
duties to each other, their God, and their new land. They were devoted to
God and to each other to make this unique experiment in government
and freedom a success. The traditions of civility and responsibility of the
public philosophy were clear and admirable.

We need to glean inspiration and guidance from our heritage and our
ancestors. Their original vision for America should still be alive today. At
times, we have heard people or politicians refer to their ideas. Ronald
Reagan referred to America as the "City on the Hill" many times during
his presidency, and Clinton referred to the covenant government makes
with its citizens in his 1992 campaign for president. Although the con-
cepts linger, most Americans have lost touch with the original idealism
and innocence of our Pilgrim ancestors. In the last thirty years schools
have failed to communicate the history of this period accurately; they
have failed to properly impart to students the enthusiastic, inspirational,
and godly fervor of our first ancestors. The Pilgrims determination and
commitment to God and each other was so strong that they did not quit
and go back to England after many of the colonists in Plymouth died
during their first winter. The hope and vision in their hearts could not be

extinguished by any amount of suffering. They were determined to bring glory to God in this new land and finally have an opportunity to worship God in their own manner.

We find this same kind of resolve in all immigrants who have come to America. Throughout the years, immigrants have continued to manifest the same kind of determination found in our first forefathers. However, these heroic ancestors have more than the quality of determination to offer us. They also had a commitment to practice justice, mercy, and love towards their neighbors. They made a covenant with each other to help everyone in their community survive and prosper. They formed a government in which all members had an opportunity to influence decisions. From these local governments came the town hall meetings in which direct democracy was practiced. And, by the time of the Founding Fathers, the practice of democracy initiated by the early colonists laid the foundation for our republican democracy. The Puritans and Pilgrims are the ancestors of all Americans, not because we are descended from them by blood. They are our ancestors because our idealistic dreams, form of government, vision, and unquenchable optimism began with them. They are the spiritual parents of our hope to be the best that humanity can be. They expressed the idealistic desire to be a good country and a good people, and that desire should never die.

The Founding Fathers: The Founding Fathers held to most of the same virtues as the Pilgrims/Puritans even though they modified some of the more strict interpretations of their customs and practices. Even the founders who were not Christians were saturated with the Christian worldview. Jefferson, a Deist who did not believe Jesus was the Son of God, felt the teachings of Jesus were the most complete expression of moral principles ever taught. He used the direct teachings of Jesus as his moral guide.[8]

The founders of our system of government were as idealistic and hopeful as the Pilgrims/Puritans. They exuded a sense of confidence that a God or Providence had called them to a task important for all mankind. As quoted earlier, Benjamin Franklin saw the American cause as "the cause of all mankind,..."9 They were given a special responsibility to create what they saw as the first true democracy, assuring freedom and equality. Their goal was to establish a government in which the majority of the public would rule. The people would be free from domination by one ruler, a monarch, or the rule of a few, an oligarchy. Their greatest fear was that their experiment would fail because of the weaknesses of human nature in all humans. Repeatedly our forefathers warned us to stay strongly committed to the public philosophy:

*No free government, nor the blessings of liberty can be preserved to any people except by a firm adherence to justice, moderation, temperance, frugality, and virtue. (George Mason)*10

*May God give us wisdom, fortitude, perseverance and every other virtue necessary for us to maintain that independence which we have asserted. (Samuel Adams)*11

Freedom is now in your power. Value the heavenly gift. Remember, if you dare to neglect or despise it, you offer an insult to the Divine Bestower. (John Jay) 12

*How vain are laws without manners. These cannot be expected unless the strictest attention is paid to the education of youth and the inculcation of true love and the fear of the Supreme Being. (John Dickenson)*13

These are only a few of the thousands of quotations one could find expressing the importance of the public philosophy to our Founding

Fathers. They knew the Union was a gift from God or a Supreme Being, and they did their utmost to build into the Constitution the means to preserve it. They knew they could not depend only on people or politicians acting out of good motives. They hoped citizens would receive the training and education to assure their goodness, but they also built into the government system the checks and balances to protect it from the natural tendency of humans to become corrupted.

Our founders were mainly motivated from pure hearts to create this unique government of the United States of America. They are one of the examples from the past to which Americans must turn. As Machiavelli said, we need to look back to our forefathers, the Pilgrims/Puritans and our Founding Fathers, to find the original vision and innocence that will inspire us to restore our nation to its traditions of civility and the rule of the people. American citizens no longer rule, and their power can only be restored by their adopting the public philosophy, which will restore their virtue.

In the following statement, authored eleven years before the Constitution of the United States was written, John Adams speculated in a letter about what it would take to create a government by the people.

The form of government which you admire, when its principles are pure, is admirable indeed. It is productive of everything which is great and excellent among men. But its principles are as easily destroyed as human nature is corrupted. Such a government is only to be supported by pure religion or austere morals. Public virtue cannot exist in a nation without private [virtue]; and public virtue is the only foundation of republics. There must be a positive passion for the public good, the public interest, honor, power, and glory established in the minds of the people, or there can be no republican government, nor any real liberty. (John Adams) [14]

By looking back to our ancestors, Americans can draw on their values to reestablish their own virtuous principles. Citizens of the revolutionary and constitutional period agreed to the rightness of the ethical principles of trustworthiness, responsibility, love, respect, patience, kindness, honesty, faithfulness, and loyalty, to name only a few. As mentioned earlier, the same duties imposed upon citizens were also imposed upon property owners and public servants. The traditions of civility included etiquette, manners, customs, norms, and moral teachings. Although these were not perfect societies (and there will never be a perfect society), they were societies that assured order, respect, strong families, and a government ruled by the people. Today very little of those four characteristics remain. It is the duty of Americans to reinstate the traditions of civility that were abandoned in the 1960s and 1970s. What was lost can be regained by understanding what caused our downfall and by taking responsibility to correct our mistakes and indiscretions.

Other Consequences Of Having Few Traditions Of Civility

Another consequence of being without traditions of civility is our increased failure to produce reflective, mature individuals who can maintain a free society. Children who are neglected are less able to acquire the "higher, more reflective mental qualities" that are required in a democratic republic. When problems arise, a reflective person is able to be objective under stress and not allow emotions to overtake them. Moreover, they have the ability to empathize with others. Empathy develops "only in a baby who has the chance to interact routinely and consistently with an admiring, supportive caregiver in a relationship that provides security and intimacy."[15] Stanley Greenspan says in his book, *The Growth of the Mind*, that neglected or abused children; "children whose parents are so caught up with meeting their own needs that they are unable to feel for their child; even children whose parents are devoted and protective but are so busy that they have no time left for exchanges of feelings—all are at grave risk for not fully realizing their humanity."[16]

When children do not have the emotional experience to assure proper mental development, their lack of humanity can undermine civil behavior. Children who have not developed empathy and moral qualities will "act impulsively, think in rigid and polarized terms, fall short in nuance and subtlety, and ignore the rights, needs, and dignity of others. Should the number of such people grow, we would expect society to become more unpredictable and dangerous, with rising violence and anti-social behavior and less self-restraint and negotiation."[17] These are not just fears projected into the future. We see these behaviors have already increased in the last twenty years.

Parents have to return to the traditional norms of the public philosophy that places the highest value on parenting. Many Americans are neglecting their children. Good parenting assures the existence of a good society by producing responsible, civil citizens. The standard for parenting does not need to exclusively place the woman as the at-home parent. There has been some positive questioning of roles in the family that should be integrated into the public philosophy model. The Judeo-Christian and natural law principles establish the need for parents to love, nourish, train, and discipline their children. Neutral or positive cultural changes can modify moral principles as long as the ultimate goals of the principles are fulfilled. Parents have been given the weighty responsibility to raise children with good character who have a heart to serve others and their civil society; parents can be creative in achieving that goal.

What Must The American Public Do To Save The Republic?

The American public has the authority to rule this nation, but citizens are not using their authority. They are not ruling because they have allowed their public opinion to be managed by different groups using the media.

As noted earlier, the tragedy in Littleton and the Lewinsky scandal were opportunities for Americans to face the moral problems in this nation. Because they no longer had the tools of the public philosophy, the traditions of civility, to apply to the problems, they decided to ignore and deny the truth. They let Clinton and other liberal politicians distract them to more acceptable reasons for the crimes. Since the public had adapted to having its opinion formed by the media, people no longer wanted the responsibility for guiding their representatives. They especially wanted to stay in denial since they had lost sight of the values that would have given them the answers to these problems.

In addition, since the consciences of American citizens have no longer been tuned to the public philosophy, they do not have the capacity for outrage for civil injustices and political betrayal. Outrage is saved mainly for personal or family injustices. If an individual or someone in his/her family is hurt or killed, immediate outrage leads to the forming of some group to help other families with the same tragedy. The public has been conditioned to respond to personal concerns more than political ones. They are trained to think subjectively or personally rather than objectively. Therefore, they have trouble identifying and feeling anger towards political or governmental indiscretions.

The desire to live in denial is common when a person or group is in a state of confusion or in a state of stress. As mentioned earlier, in the 1970s I became a part of a Christian cult because I could no longer find direction in my life. I was not conscious that the undermining of the public philosophy, which was uprooting all of society, was leaving me without a moral anchor and sense of order. Therefore, I looked for someone to give me answers rather than searching for answers myself. In the end, when I left the church, I felt I had to blame myself more than the leader for having been deceived. I had already deceived myself as to my reasons for joining the church before he was able to deceive me. I should have taken responsibility to define my own goals and give my life meaning. Even though the pastor acted immorally and deceptively, I had to face up to the fact that it was my own irresponsible behavior that set me up to be controlled and manipulated. The choice I made to face my responsibility for being deceived and controlled is the choice many Americans need to make in their own deceived and controlled state.

The public needs to become the public again instead of the masses. We need take back the responsibility to rule our nation. In order to achieve this goal, we will have to return to an absolute code for moral behavior. The culture needs to be restored to the public philosophy. We need to take responsibility to know what is wrong with our government, society, education, and morality. Then, we have to find a way to make our government more responsive to us again.

Americans need to decide to take back their consciences, their minds, and their souls. The first step is to recommit to absolute moral principles. Moral relativism has completely devastated the American culture and moral system. Moral, universal principles provide societies with common norms and a basis for trust. They redirect people's attention away from themselves to others. They tell us that our best actions are those that help others and contribute to society. We realize that our most important reason for being alive is to contribute our talents and abilities to better the lives of others. They tell us to be honest and not lie, cheat, or steal. They tell us to put our family, community, and nation before ourselves. Without moral absolutes, a nation has no grounds for unity or trust, and people have no guide for their consciences. Society has trouble functioning in a civilized manner when there are no moral absolutes.

Frances Fukuyama, a modern thinker, points out the weaknesses in liberal democracies. He is also concerned about how to "re-norm" societies. He sees that the norms provided by liberal ideas have not yet succeeded in repairing the disruption caused by the Information Age. He notes that "…social and moral order do not necessarily follow in the wake of political order and economic development." In addition, "The moral guidelines a liberal society provides are universal obligations for tolerance and mutual respect."[18] These guidelines are not sufficient to unite people in a heterogeneous society. He goes on to state that the splintering in American society is caused not only by limited guidelines and diversity but also by "…the spread of a principled belief in moral relativism—the idea that no particular set of values or norms can or ought to be authoritative. When this relativism extends to the political values on which the regime itself is based, then liberalism begins to undermine itself."[19]

These insights lead us back to the conclusion that the answer to the present deterioration of our society is for us to restore moral absolutes. Moral absolutes are part of the public philosophy, which our heritage has provided for our edification. It has only been forty years since we believed in these absolutes. Many of us were alive in the 1940s and 1950s and know how to return to them. These values were the ones to which Kennedy was pointing. He was turning us away from the trend towards selfishness.

Some people may criticize the idea that Kennedy was restoring us to the traditions of civility. They would question Kennedy's own moral behavior. Since he did not always obey moral absolutes, how could he be a voice to restore them? In the case of Kennedy, we know he followed the civil application of the public philosophy. He saw the need for honorable, public service. In his private life, we can only conclude from the books written about him that he fell short of living up to the traditions of civility. It is common for humans, being fallible, to believe in what is morally right but not always live by what they believe. Therefore, it should be our goal to surpass his example of a life conformed to the public philosophy. We should endeavor to be more consistent in our efforts to develop good character. But we should not ignore the idealistic political and social message that came out of Kennedy's heart. He was a man for his time. He had an idea whose time had come. He reminded us that all citizens in a democracy needed to serve in some manner. He was reminding us it was time to restore the ideal of public service.

What Specific Areas Of Resistance Would There Be To Moral Absolutes?

What could prevent us from returning to moral absolutes? Mainly our desires to do what we want when we want to. We have become attuned to putting our own needs first and to frequently following our instincts. A case in point is that the freedom many Americans have exercised in sexual pursuits will have to be curbed. Will people be willing to accept sexual morality as a condition to restore the public philosophy? Some would say sex outside of marriage is an exception to the traditions of civility. Such a belief would be hard to prove. Sexual immorality leads to other immoral decisions that further undermine the public philosophy. It would be difficult to line up the principles of trustworthiness, loyalty, respect, honor, self-control, love, responsibility, and honesty with sexual freedom. Too many of these principles are broken when there is sex outside of marriage.

People need to be open to rethink sexual issues in order to restore the traditions of civility. If we retain our present sexual attitudes, too many exceptions would have to be made to those traditions, and we would soon be back to where we started. Surprisingly, sex is probably the one area in which there would be the most resistance. Possibly, the area of family responsibility would also rise up. Many women want to stay in the work place even though it is hurting their children. Would a majority of married couples be willing to adjust their lifestyles to fulfill their responsibilities to their children as defined by the public philosophy? Are they willing to sacrifice their own desires for the welfare of their children?

There would be other areas of resistance to the public philosophy. Corporate heads would probably resist a return to the public philosophy because their work force would be diminished. If more men and women decide to spend more hours at home, it will deplete the number of employees available to work. Also, many liberal groups would feel attacked and condemned for their behavior. Liberal special interests would have to decide to put the good of the country, at least in some important instances, before their own agendas. In addition, they would have to give up using deception and dishonesty to promote their causes. Many of the moderate Republicans and Democrats would probably resist because they have lost sight of traditional values. They would have to begin thinking of making decisions for the common good and according to conscience rather than for special interests or personal gain. All the campaign finance laws would have to be changed to bring government control back to the people. The Conservative Republicans might accept the idea, but they would have to separate themselves from some of the economic ideals that overprotect corporations. In conclusion, all factions would need to adopt the public philosophy as their guide.

The Need For A Third Party Or A Transformation In One Of The Traditional Parties

Neither the Republican or Democratic Parties have the answers and vision that our country needs. The Republicans are more connected to the capitalist elite; and the Democrats are controlled by liberal coalitions, and from all appearances, the corporate elite as well. Each party would have to relinquish its undemocratic coalitions, restoring healthy factionalism to special interests. It would be surprising if either party was willing to inspire and lead the nation back to the public philosophy. Both the capitalist philosophy and romantic liberalism have faulty ideas, but the basis of the liberal one, human nature is good, leads to the greatest destruction of civilized society. Modern liberalism has to be replaced by some blend of liberalism based on the truth about human nature. Its faulty premises lead to faulty conclusions and actions. The liberal falsehoods have severely and negatively changed the American culture, and the logical progression of its

main principle will, in time, totally separate us from the roots of our original culture and government.

The Conservative group in the Republican Party could possibly take
on the job of moving the nation to the traditions of civility. They have
failed so far because they have focused on individual issues—abortion,
education, and gay rights—rather than on the bigger picture. They have
also appeared too emotional. In addition, they will need to commit to
civil conservatism and reject the economic conservatism of big business.
If the Conservatives form their own party or take control of the
Republican Party, they will have to live by the public philosophy not the
philosophy of the power elite if they are to be successful in reforming
American culture.

If a third party does not come out of the traditional parties, one will
have to be created to restore the public philosophy. The Reform Party
made an effort to bring some reforms, but internal strife and stereotyping
by its opponents have made it ineffective. Once a third party is established, one of the other two parties would ultimately be replaced by the
third party. In the end, the people at the grassroots level may lead the
party rather than the party lead the people. The Civil Rights Movement
was an example of the process of grassroots leadership. It is difficult to
know the conclusion of the efforts to restore the traditions of civility. It
will be up to the American public and visionary, sacrificial leadership to
return the nation to the public philosophy and restore the government to
popular rule.

What Is Being Asked Of All Americans

What is being asked of all Americans—every special interest and every
person in this nation—is to make a decision based on what is good, not
for themselves first, but what is good for the society as a whole, the common good. Citizens need to stop putting themselves first, and, instead,

put the good of others and this nation above their own desires, pleasures, and goals. I am putting forth this challenge to the citizens, political activists, and politicians to restore their consciences, adopt the traditions of civility, and serve their families and the public for the sake of the dream of our Puritan ancestors and the vision of our Founding Fathers. Let us not let their sacrifices, inspirational ideals, and hard work be in vain. Let us not forget all of the children who have been dying from mass killings by other children. Let not their deaths be in vain.

We have a responsibility to those who have gone before, to those who are presently suffering, and to the generations of Americans to come to choose to seek the common good. We must wrench ourselves from the hold of self and all of its demands. We must rise above all that drags our souls into the mud of self-interest and self-love. There is a better way. John F. Kennedy presented a vision of public service, duty, courage, and unselfishness. He came to remind us that there is more to life than material things and pleasure. We are humans and not animals. Let us return to our humanity and to the human examples of the past who modeled the best that humans could become. Let us return to the fork in the road, November 22, 1963. This time let us take the road of the public philosophy and not the road of self-interest and self-love. Let us fulfill the legacy of Kennedy, which was built on the traditions of our founders, for the sake of preserving the most successful government the world has ever known.

There is placed before us an unreachable goal—an ideal of service, duty and love. This ideal tells us what we are supposed to be. It has been placed out of reach so that we will endeavor to achieve the greatest potential of our higher nature. Tragically, this standard was lowered for Americans, and we have been expected to achieve only the potential of our lower, instinctual nature. We now declare that we reject this offense to our humanity. We declare, "We are more than animals; we are humans." The Creator and natural law confirm that we can ascend above our lower nature and love more than ourselves. We here decide to endeavor to fulfill the ideal of love and service, knowing we will at times fall short. Nevertheless, we determine to refuse to let failure stop us from reasserting again our undiminished effort to complete the calling that is on our lives—the calling to contribute to our families, neighbors, communities, and nation. We choose to restore to our nation the public philosophy and renew the initial godly covenant upon which America was founded.

Notes

Chapter 1

The Demise of American Culture

1. Lipmann, *The Public Philosophy*. Quoted in Brown, *Great American Political Thinkers*, 394.
2. Aaseng, *Great Decision Series. You Are The President*, 99-100.
3. Mills, *The Power Elite*, 310.
4. Lippmann, *The Public Philosophy*, in Brown, *Great American Political Thinkers*, 404.
5. Madison, *Federalist Papers*, (No. 51), 322.
6. Letters of John Adams: John Adams to Samuel Adams, New York, 18 October 1790.
7. Jefferson, *The Life and Selected Writings of Thomas Jefferson*. To Peter Carr, pages 373-374.
8. Franklin, *Autobiography. Poor Richard Letters*. Quoted in Carlsen, *American Literature* pages 94-95.
9. Franklin in a letter to Henry Home of Kames, quoted from "Memoirs of the Life and Writings of the Honourable Henry Home of Kames," Vol. 1, 268.
10. Lippmann, *The Public Philosophy*, in *Great American Political Thinkers*, ed. Brown, 400.
11. Ibid., 403.
12. Ibid., 404.
13. Adams, *Writings of Samuel Adams*. Quoted in Richards, *God of Our Fathers*, 193.

14. Lippmann, *The Public Philosophy*, in *Great Political Thinkers*, ed. Brown, 397.

15. Ibid., 397-398.

16. Goldwater, *Conscience of a Conservative*, 6.

Chapter 2

Kennedy's Death Unleashes Liberal Excesses

1. Madison, Federalist Papers, (No. 51), 322.

2. Ibid.

3. Madison, *James Madison, A Biography in His Own Words*, ed. Peterson 148.

4. Madison, *Federalist Papers*, (No. 51), 324.

5. Ibid., 324.

6. Mills, *Power Elite*, 18.

7. Ibid., 20.

8. Lippmann, in *Great Political Thinkers*, ed. Brown, 394, 400.

9. Mills, *Power Elite*, 20.

10. Smith, *The Shaping of America: A People's History of the Young Republic*. Vol. 3, 82..

11. Kennedy, *Profiles in Courage*, 258.

Chapter 3

The Culture That Used To Be

1. Confucius, *The Wisdom of China and India*, 845.

2. Toqueville, *Democracy in America*, 33.

3. Ibid., 46.

4. Hirsch, The *Schools We Need*, 73.
5. Confucius, *Wisdom of China*, 838.
6. Ibid., 846.
7. From a survey by The Joseph & Edna Josephson Institute of Ethics, 1992. 4640 Admiralty Way, Suite 1002, Marina del Rey, CA 90292. (310-306-1868).

Chapter 4

The Big Bang Cultural Transformation

1. Hirsch, *Schools We Need*, 75.
2. Ibid.
3. Berlin, *The Age of Enlightenment*, 14.
4. From a speech entitled, "Experiments in Moral Education," made by William Kilpatrick, professor in the School of Education at Boston College, November 1997, page 2. Reference: online at http://www.hi-ho.ne.jp/taku77/refer/kilpat.htm
5. Ibid., 3.
6. Hewlett, *The War Against Parents*, 135.
7. Schoeck, *Envy: A Theory of Social Behaviour,"* 33.
8. Ibid.

Chapter 5

Special Interests Contribute to the Demise of American Culture

1. Quoted in Richards, *God of Our Fathers*, 53.
2. Quoted in Richards, God of Our Fathers, 105.

3. Paula Martinac, "Gay Marriage," *San Jose Mercury News*, 11 July 1999, Perspective.

4. Ibid., all other quotations from Paula Martinac are from this article.

5. Michael Weis, "Carter's Malaise Speech Was Dead-On," San Jose Mercury News, 11 July 1999, Perspective.

6. Ibid.

7. Smith, *The New Age Now Begins*. Vol. 1, 159.

Chapter 6

The Media: Tool for Deception

1. Mills, *Power Elite*, 316.

2. Joel Brinkley, San Jose Mercury News, 18 September 1999, Perspective.

3. Ibid.

4. Ohmann, Richard, "Doublespeak and Ideology in Ads: A Kit for Teachers," in Lazere, *American Media and Mass Culture*, 108-109.

5. King, Jr., *A Testament of Hope: The Essential Writings of Martin Luther King, Jr.*, ed. James M. Washington, 88.

6. Ibid.

Chapter 7

Liberal Education Has Undermined the Public Philosophy

1. Smith, *The Shaping of America*.Vol. 3, 352.

2. Madison, *Madison, A Biography in His own Words*, ed. Peterson. 379-380.

3. Ibid.

4. Jefferson, Quoted in Richards, *God of Our Fathers*, 230-231.

5. Jefferson, *The Life and Selected Writings*, 264.
6. Smith, *The Shaping of America*, Vol. 3, 360.
7. Smith, *The Rise of Industrial America*, Vol. 6, 594.
8. Ibid., 601.
9. Ibid., 599.
10. Hirsch, *The Schools We Need*, 2.
11. Mills, *The Power Elite*, 318.
12. Clinton, *It Takes A Village*, 211.

Chapter 8.

Old and New Morality

1. Aristotle, *The Politics*, 59.
2. Aristotle, 60.
3. Ibid., 95.
4. The New Testament (NAB), Philippians, Chapter 2:34.
5. Robert M. Stein, "Sexuality, Shadow, and the Holy Bible," found in *The Shadow in America*, ed. Abrams, 123.
6. Ibid., 124.

Chapter 9

The Failure of Churches to Maintain the Public Philosophy

1. Miller, *The Puritans*, Vol. 1, 143-144.
2. Marshall, *The Light and the Glory*, 120.
3. Miller, 198.
4. O'Connor, *Religion and American Society*, 144.
5. Ibid.

6. O'Connor, 177.
7. The Old Testament (NAB), Jeremiah, Chapter 17:4.
8. Fromm, *Escape from Freedom*, 93.
9. Hewlett, *The War Against Parents*, 32-33.

Chapter 10

What It Will Take to Restore American Culture

1. Toqueville, *Democracy in America*, 45.
2. Machiavelli, *The Portable Machiavelli*, ed. and trans. Bondanella, 351.
3. Ibid., 225.
4. Miller, *The Puritans*, 147-148.
5. Ibid., 152.
6. Miller, 198.
7. Ibid., 199.
8. Jefferson, *The Life and Selected Writings of Thomas Jefferson*, 632.
9. Richards, *God of our Fathers*, 53.
10. Richards, 37.
11. Richards, 43.
12. Richards, 49.
13. Richards, 107.
14. Richards, 34.
15. Greenspan, *The Growth of the Mind*, 119.
16. Ibid.
17. Ibid., 308.
18. Fukuyama, *The Great Disruption*, 281.
19. Ibid., 28.

Bibliography

Abrams, Jermiah., ed. *The Shadow in America*. Novato: Nataraj Publishing, 1994.

Aaseng, Nathan. *Great Decision Series: You Are the President*. Minneapolis: Oliver Press, 1994.

Aristotle. *The Politics*. New York: Penquin Books, 1981.

Berlin, Sir Isaiah. *The Age of Enlightenment*. New York: Penguin Books, 1984.

Brown, Bernard E., ed. *Great American Political Thinkers: Modern America Since the Civil War and Industrialism*. Vol. 2. New York: Avon Books, 1983.

Clinton, Hillary Rodham. *It Takes A Village: And Other Lesson Children Teach Us*. New York: Touchstone, 1996.

Ebenstein, William, and Alan O. Ebenstein. *Great Political Thinkers: Plato to the Present*.

Forth Worth: Holt, Rinehart and Winston, Inc., 1991.

Carlsen, Robert G., et. al. *American Literature*. New York: Webster Division, McGraw Hill, 1985.

Fromm, Erich. *Escape from Freedom*. New York:Avon Books, 1969.

Fukuyama, Francis. *The Great Disruption*. New York: The Free Press, 1999.

Goldwater, Barry. *The Conscience of a Conservative*. Washington, DC: Regnery, Gateway, Inc., 1990.

Greenspan, Stanley I. *The Growth of the Mind:And the Endangered Origins of Intelligence*. Menlo Park: Addison-Wesley, 1996.

Hewlett, Sylvia Ann, and Cornel West. *The War Against Parents: What We Can Do for America's Beleaguered Moms and Dads*. Boston: Houghton, 1998.

Hirsch, Jr., E.D. *The Schools We Need: Why We Don't Have Them.* New York: Doubleday, 1996.

Hamilton, Alexander, and James Madison, and John Jay. *The Federalist Papers*, ed. Clinton Rossiter. New York: Mentor Book, 1961.

Jefferson, Thomas. "Notes on Virginia" and "Letters Of." In *The Life and Selected Writings of Thomas Jefferson*, ed. A. Koch and W. Peden. New York: Random House, 1972.

Kennedy, John F. *Profiles in Courage.* New York: Harper Perennial, 1956.

King, Jr. Martin Luther. *A Testament of Hope: The Essential Writings of Martin Luther King, Jr.*, ed. James M. Washington. San Francisco: Harper & Row, 1986.

Lazere, Donald, ed. *American Media and Mass Culture.* Berkeley and Los Angeles: University of California Press, 1987.

Machiavelli, Niccolo di Bernardo. *The Portable Machiavelli*, ed. and trans., Peter Bondanella and Mark Musa. NewYork: Penguin, 1979.

Madison, James. *James Madison, A Biography in His Own Words*, ed. Merril D. Peterson.

Newsweek Book Division, 1974.

Marshall, Peter, and David Manuel. *The Light and the Glory.* Old Tappan: Fleming H. Revell Company, 1977.

Miller, Perry, and Thomas H. Johnson. *The Puritans.* Vol. 1. New York: Harper & Row, 1963.

Mills, C. Wright. *The Power Elite.* London: Oxford UP, 1956.

O'Connor, Thomas H. *Religion and American Society.* Menlo Park: Addison-Wesley, 1975.

Richards, Josiah Benjamin, comp. and ed. *God of our Fathers.* Reading: Reading Books, 1994.

Schoeck, Helmut. *Envy: A Theory of Social Behaviour.* Indianapolis: Liberty Press, 1987.

Smith, Page. *The New Age Begins: The People's History of the American Revolution*. Vol. 1. New York: Penguin Books, 1989.

—.*A New Age Begins: The People's History of the American Revolution*. Vol. 2. New York: Penguin Books, 1989.

—.*The Shaping of America: A People's History of the Young Republic*. Vol. 3. New York: Penguin Books, 1989.

—.*The Nation Comes of Age: A People's History of the Ante-Bellum Years*. Vol. 4.New York: Penguin Books, 1989.

—.*The Rise of Industrial America: A People's History of the Post-Reconstruction*

Era. Vol. 6. New York. Penguin Books, 1989.

Toqueville, Alexis de. *Democracy in America*. New York: Vantage Books, 1945.

Yutang, Lin., ed. *The Wisdom of China and India*. New York: The Modern Library, 1942.